Michael Clarke grew up Sydney's south west. He cracked the New South Wales team at 18 and won a Test berth in 2004, scoring 151 not out on debut. In 2011, Clarke became the 43rd captain of the Australian Test team, as well as taking the reins as leader of the Australian one-day side. In 105 Tests he has scored over 8000 runs at an average over 51 with 27 centuries. The most recent of those tons was perhaps his most famous, a fighting knock of 161 not out that clinched a 2–1 series win against South Africa and returned Australia to the summit of Test cricket as the number one team in the world. *Captain's Diary* is his second book.

Also by Michael Clarke
The Ashes Diary

Captain's Diary

MICHAEL CLARKE

Captain's Diary

MACMILLAN
Pan Macmillan Australia

First published 2014 in Macmillan by Pan Macmillan Australia Pty Ltd
1 Market Street, Sydney, New South Wales Australia 2000

Reprinted 2014, 2015

Cataloguing-in-Publication entry is available
from the National Library of Australia:
http://catalogue.nla.gov.au

The Publisher acknowledges the trademarks of Cricket
Australia in these pages and where used note that they have
been reproduced with the approval of Cricket Australia.

Typeset in 13/18.5pt Bembo by Midland Typesetters, Australia
Printed by McPherson's Printing Group

To my wife, family, fans and teammates – all of whom play a special role in my success.

Contents

Foreword by Shane Warne   xi

1   Introduction   1

2   The First Test match   15

3   The Second Test match   57

4   The Third Test match   97

5   The Fourth Test match   153

6   The Fifth Test match   199

7   Afterword by Kyly Clarke   237

8   Conclusions   243

Captain's Dossier   275

Acknowledgements   289

Foreword by Shane Warne

The first time I was introduced to Michael Clarke I knew we were kindred spirits.

It was North Sydney Oval 2003. Michael had a sparkler in his ear, a huge smile on his face – and an enormous amount of product in his hair! – but I sensed straight away that here was a man in a hurry.

Our friendship grew from that moment and ten years on we are like brothers.

The qualities that first struck me about Michael were the respect he had for the game of cricket and his hunger to learn. But it was when I saw him with a bat in his hands for the first time, playing county cricket for Hampshire in 2004, that I truly knew he was something special.

Forward or back, Michael possessed elegance. He was right at home against the speed merchants – driving, cutting and hooking. And against spin he gave a master-class in batting, with a quick mind and nimble feet that confirmed him as a player with class.

He showed that day the trait that all great batsmen do – *he had time to play.*

So when Michael made his Test debut at Bangalore in India in the 2004 series, I knew he was ready. I had the honour of presenting Michael with his baggy green cap, which made me feel very proud and he went on to make 151, still one of his career-best knocks.

Fast forward ten years and 'Pup' was barking orders as Australian captain in the 2014 Ashes series.

'Pup' is the nickname we gave Michael when he first came into the Test squad. But Pup can bite! Just ask England swing bowler James Anderson who, in the First Ashes Test in Brisbane, was on the receiving end of Pup's combative late-in-the-day bomb: 'Get ready for a broken *bleeping* arm.'

This was the moment I believe Australia saw the very competitive, tough Michael Clarke I know, and accepted him as an Australian hero.

One of the things I believe in any sport is that it's not about your stats, it's about the *way* you play the game. In cricket, what matters most is *when* you make your runs or take your wickets.

Michael Clarke has always delivered when the team most needs him to.

His recent unbeaten 161 in Cape Town, with the series ledger at 1–1 and the Third Test on the line, epitomised old-fashioned Aussie guts and determination (even though I missed the last ten runs of his century when I fell asleep in the change room!). That innings – played with a fractured shoulder against the full might of the South African pace attack – summed up how much playing for Australia means to Michael Clarke. It was a captain's knock that inspired the team to win a memorable series.

Yet something a lot of people might not be aware of is how tough Michael is.

During a Test series, Pup's day starts many hours before the rest of the team get up for breakfast. The daily exercise routine he goes through, alone and with the physios, to get that dodgy back of his right for every day's play shows an incredible commitment to the cause.

As a captain, Michael Clarke is, in my eyes, easily the best tactician in the world right now. He has flair and a real feel for the game. For a lot of us old fellas, he captains in an old-school way – by raw instinct and with great imagination . . . even if he does have his life story tattooed all over his arms!

That story now includes the tale of Michael leading Australia back to being the number one team in the world.

A lot of people have contributed to this, but none more than Captain Clarke.

Congrats on *Captain's Diary* and for all you've done for the Aussie team, my friend – long may you continue to lead the boys well. I love ya to bits!

Your friend,
Shane

1

INTRODUCTION

Sunday 17 November. **Brisbane.**

The first day of the summer! There are few days more exciting for me than this, when the cricketers lucky enough to have been chosen in the Australian team for the First Test in Brisbane come together. Early this afternoon, the boys began to arrive at our hotel, the Mantra at Southbank, where we've stayed the past few years.

It's a bit like a reunion, because we've been all around the country playing Sheffield Shield and before that, for some of the team, in the one-day international series in India. Some of us have been in Brisbane preparing at the National Cricket Centre. There's a great atmosphere around the group as we see each other again, as there is every season during this special period in Brisbane.

But this time is also different because a few months ago we were in England battling against the same opponent we're about to take on here. The winter Ashes is so recent, we don't need to talk about unfinished business. We *know* it.

I've been up in Brisbane for most of the week and it's been an interesting time. We have had a special camp for the bowlers, in which we've gone through our specific plans for every English batsman in fine detail. We followed our plans pretty well at times in the series in England, but home conditions will be different and the opposition will feature some new batsmen. Also, we will have some changes in our attack. So we have been analysing and discussing the English players, from one to eleven, and working out how to bowl at them. In some ways it's quite general: we will attack the stumps with the new ball, and when we're bowling at the tail, we'll pursue an aggressive plan, aiming to have them caught close in and behind the wicket. For individuals, in some cases it's going to be a matter of pursuing plans that worked quite well in England, such as targeting Jonathan Trott with the short ball and bowling to Alastair Cook so that we are forcing him to play in the zones where he's not used to scoring a lot of runs. By contrast, with Ian Bell our plans didn't work so successfully in England, so we have had to rethink things. For him, we have to be disciplined and not lose patience, and not give him easy runs in his favoured area wide of the off stump. We also have to tailor our plans to the different conditions. Not only will Australian wickets be different from the slow, dry surfaces we played on in the Test matches in England, but there are specific characteristics to each of the Australian venues. All will require their own adjustments.

Whoever is selected in the batting line-up, we know how vital it is to attack them early. Touring batsmen thrive on the confidence that they establish at the beginning of a series. The flipside is that if they don't make runs in the first Test or two, the pressure can build up and be hard to overcome. Touring can be very hard when you are lacking confidence. If all goes well for us, England's batsmen will have a tough time in Australia as a result of all the planning we've been doing.

Once all the boys had arrived at the Mantra today, we had team recovery and rehab sessions and personal screenings with the physio, Alex Kountouris, and the team doctor, Peter Brukner. Alex and Doc were among the support staff during our winter Ashes tour, and have been with the Australian team for a long time, so they are familiar faces. We also had a meeting to welcome some new(ish) faces, who have been brought back into the team fold, such as Craig McDermott, returning as Test match bowling coach, and Mike Young, our long-time fielding coach, whose inspirational message I carry with me at all times, taped to the lining of my bag:

'A *professional* is . . . One who competes against the challenges brought before him by others and is willing to test himself each and every day to be the best *he* can possibly be and *not* the best others feel he should be!'

They are words I try to live by every day, and it's great to have Mike back. We also welcomed Damien Mednis as strength and conditioning coach. Damien is a big Queenslander and a true professional whom most of us have known for a fair while.

After those formalities, we had a really enjoyable team dinner at a Turkish restaurant across the road from the hotel, in the Southbank nightlife precinct. There was a happy mood at the table. Everyone's champing at the bit for our first training session tomorrow.

Since finishing my diary of the Ashes series in England, I've had some ups and downs with my back. I stayed for the full seven-match limited-overs series in England, and had a great time. We won, which was a nice boost to our confidence after not beating England in a single Test match in the Ashes series, and we also made some important new discoveries. George Bailey was in commanding form, scoring runs at will, as he has done during the last couple of seasons in our one-day and Twenty20 teams. Just as importantly, he proved he was extremely comfortable in the international arena. Shane Watson had a good series, carrying over his form from the Test matches, and I made a few scores too. The revelation was Mitchell Johnson, who gave some of the English batsmen, notably Jonathan Trott and Kevin Pietersen, all sorts of difficulties with his pace and hostility. Mitch has been doing a lot of work on his bowling quietly, away from the limelight, and he has a whole new aura about him. In fact, at the team announcement I predicted that Mitch will be man of the Ashes series. Let's see! When he joined us for the one-dayers in England he was a real handful, appreciably quicker than last year. He'll never be a naggingly accurate bowler in the mould of Peter Siddle, but the flipside is that he can bowl so fast, with so many potentially wicket-taking balls, that he will be genuinely frightening for some batsmen. He carried that form through the one-day series in India, as did George, and both of them have been chosen in our Test twelve here in Brisbane. Those two aside, we are all returning players from the last Ashes Test match at the Oval.

After winning the one-day series in England, we came home feeling good, but I had to get some intensive treatment on my back injury and my body as a whole, so I didn't go to India. The boys played very well again under George's captaincy, and while they didn't win the series they pushed the world's number one limited-overs team right to the wire.

Meanwhile, I was ready to recommence competitive cricket at the start of the New South Wales Blues' Sheffield Shield campaign in early November. I had received more treatment in October during the Ryobi Cup domestic limited-overs series, but had not been fit to play for the

Blues, who reached the final at North Sydney Oval but unfortunately were beaten by the Queensland Bulls. For four weeks I needed daily treatment, a serious rehab program for what had developed into a severe injury.

I watched with interest as some of the likely picks for our eleven for the First Test match started their seasons. Davey Warner hit a succession of hundreds for New South Wales in the Ryobi Cup and the Sheffield Shield, regaining his full quota of confidence. Ryan Harris and Peter Siddle played in the Ryobi Cup, and were steadily regaining condition and form in the early Shield rounds. Steve Smith made good runs while leading New South Wales to the Ryobi Cup final. So for a lot of the boys, it was a good reintroduction to cricket after the post-Ashes break.

Alastair Cook and the England squad arrived in Australia during this period for three lead-up first-class matches, and there was some commentary on whether we were getting as good preparation for the First Test as the English team was. The focus was on our boys playing one-day cricket in India while England were acclimatising to red-ball cricket in Australian conditions. But this commentary might have overlooked the fact that only four of what would turn out to be our Brisbane Test eleven – George Bailey, Mitchell Johnson, Shane Watson and Brad Haddin – were in India playing the one-dayers, and the rest of us were in Australia. Some of us would play in all three rounds of the Sheffield Shield at home, and the four guys returning from India would get one first-class match back at home, so in my view that was a pretty solid grounding.

Everyone had to prepare in his own way, and after so much work on my body I was ready in time for New South Wales' first match against Tasmania. My back was fine during that match and the next, against Victoria. Across the nation, the prospective Test players were scoring runs and taking wickets. Chris Rogers made a good solid start to the season, playing some long innings for Victoria, Davey Warner was churning out hundreds and some fifties, Smithy was consistent for New South Wales, and all the bowlers were building up well. Watto had strained his hamstring during the last one-day match in India and was resting up, while George Bailey, Mitch Johnson, Brad Haddin and James Faulkner, who'd also done extremely well in India, were all fit enough to get one Sheffield Shield game under their belts. There were positive signs for everyone, with bat and ball, giving us that essential confidence moving towards the First Test. In terms of preparation, we weren't giving away any advantage to England.

There's always a heightened level of expectation and speculation leading up to an Ashes series, and the only bump in the road during October was some public criticism of me through some comments in Ricky Ponting's autobiography, which came out a few weeks back. When you're Australian captain you get used to criticism.

It's part and parcel of the job. My response to this is not to try to address every little thing that is said. To me, it's irrelevant. I've got far more pressing concerns. My sole objective is to put this stuff behind me and perform on the field. All I've ever tried in my career is to do my best for the team, and that's what I'm doing now, focusing wholly and solely on preparing for the Ashes series.

So, putting that behind me, all was looking rosy when I flew up to Brisbane early last week and trained on Tuesday with the New South Wales team in preparation for our Shield match against Queensland. We had the launch of the new National Cricket Centre, and then the announcement of the Test twelve. My back felt one hundred per cent, absolutely fine. Then, on Wednesday, I had a session on my own, facing throwdowns and having an hour's batting. While I was doing that, there was that all-too-familiar grab in my back, the same old seizure that has taken place from time to time ever since I was a teenager. I saw Alex and went for a session in the pool, but the back still didn't feel right.

Thursday morning when I woke up, it was déjà vu: the same back stiffness and soreness. My movement was restricted by the pain. I used a machine in Brisbane that is similar to the MedX I worked on in Sydney and London during the past year, which anyone who read my first tour diary would be used to hearing about, so I won't go into all the painful detail about it! I also saw

Alex for more physio treatment, but the soreness didn't go away.

So on Friday we organised five cortisone injections, the same as those I had had leading up to the series in England. My back soon felt better, and I took it easy through Friday and Saturday while the cortisone was going to work. This morning I had a bat in the nets at the National Cricket Centre, and got through without any pain or restriction. So, after a tense few days, I'm happy with it again.

That is a full update on events since the end of my last Ashes Diary. To be honest, I have a feeling that the boys are flying. The mood is so good now that we are all back together. Only four sleeps until we are facing England in a Test match. It feels like just a couple of weeks ago we were playing them at the Oval. Having another Ashes series so soon after an unsuccessful one is a priceless opportunity for us. We don't have to watch England holding the Ashes for the usual two years. We can take them back now.

Monday 18 November. Brisbane.

The boys had a good night's sleep after our Turkish dinner, and we were well rested for a big day today. We had a team meeting at 7.45 am, and as I write this it's 6 pm and I have only just got back to the hotel.

For our team meeting, every player had been charged with gathering new information on one England player and outlining where we could improve our plans to counter him since the last series. My player was Steven Finn, who played in just the First Test at Nottingham, but has been brought out to Australia as one of several very tall seamers, along with Chris Tremlett and Boyd Rankin, in hopes of exploiting our bouncier wickets. The information session was useful, and most of the boys were able to make interesting contributions. We talked a lot about the role each of us will play – where we will bat, what our bowling job is, how we all fit into the cohesion of the team.

We followed that meeting with a good cardio session to blow out the cobwebs, and then went into the nets at the National Cricket Centre. Everyone has a lot of cricket under their belt, and I couldn't see anyone showing signs of rust. Our team is ready to go.

The afternoon featured a season launch for the Commonwealth Bank at Queen Street Mall, which was a bit embarrassing, as we had to walk through Brisbane's central business and shopping district dressed in our creams. It was quite funny, but people were very supportive and wanted us to sign autographs and pose with them for photos. If there's one thing about Queenslanders, when they're behind you, they're full-on about it.

So it's only now that we get to sit down. Tonight is for chilling out and doing as we please. I'm super-excited, as tomorrow we go to the Gabba for our first training session at the venue where the Test match is going to be played.

Wednesday 20 November. Brisbane.

Yesterday and today, we have been concentrating as individuals and as a team on getting what we want out of the last two training sessions. Yesterday, I made it one of my top priorities to look at the wicket and have a chat with the Gabba's curator, Kevin Mitchell Junior. From what I could see, the wicket was fairly grassy but dry underneath – certainly a different type of strip from what we saw in England over the winter months.

The flow of information in a chat with Kevin is pretty much one-way. I don't tell him anything, I just ask questions. I asked him whether he was going to mow the grass again, how he thought the wicket would play over the course of the five days, and what was the weather forecast. I don't know how it works in every other cricket country, but in Australia the home Test captain does not get any say in what wickets we get. Kevin would have started preparing this one ten days before the match, and I only see it for the first time two days before the match. There's nothing I can tell him about pitch preparation, or nothing he would listen to anyway.

Yesterday's training session was intense. Mark Taylor, the former Australian captain and now Nine Network commentator, has joined the group for these three days, and has given us some help with adjusting our alignment in the slips cordon. Under the watchful eyes of Tubby, Mike Young and Steve Rixon, our fielding and catching preparation has been as good as I could hope for.

Today, Wednesday, was more of a top-up session, for guys to sort out their final individual needs, and to go to the changing rooms and unpack our gear. There is not a lot left to do, other than fine-tune ourselves mentally. The significant part of our preparation has been completed well and truly before today.

I stayed at the Gabba to look at the pitch and take part in the traditional photo opportunity with Alastair Cook, posing with the replica Ashes urn. I'm hoping that this time the photo call is not the closest I get to the trophy.

We also had the captains' pre-match press conference, in which I gather I surprised the media crew by being quite short, even terse, in my answers. It wasn't planned. I can say that I, like everyone in our team, have had enough of the phoney war, the commentary from players, ex-players, the public, the media, everyone stirring the pot. One small comment about one player, and it's front-page news. The local newspaper, the *Courier-Mail*, has been on a campaign to get up the English players' noses, particularly targeting Kevin Pietersen and Stuart Broad, and I want no part in adding to the large and growing stock of tomorrow's fish and chips wrappers. To be frank,

I'm sick of it and just want to play now. I'm tired of waiting for the talk to stop and the cricket to start. A lot of our guys have chosen not to read what's written on the papers or websites, or to watch television coverage, and from what I've seen their media blackout has held them in good stead. We've all got to prepare mentally in our own way. I've tried to do the same, just skimming and turning the page, keeping an eye on things without getting involved in the detail, and to be honest I'm over it.

My mental preparation today has been the same as it always is before a Test match. There is always extra build-up for the Ashes, which is great for the fans and great for the game of cricket, but as a player you need to take yourself away from that a bit. I don't try any harder in the Ashes than I do in other matches for Australia. That is not to disrespect the Ashes, but my goal is to achieve performance of a certain standard, and to extract that from myself I have to prepare the same way that works for me elsewhere. So I am focusing on this series in the same way I focused against New Zealand, India, South Africa and Sri Lanka in the past two home seasons. I'm facing the red ball, not James Anderson or Stuart Broad or Graeme Swann. If you get caught up in personalities and the Ashes and the hype and everything other than that red ball, you will soon find yourself in trouble.

But I'm not an isolated individual either; I'm a member of this team. There are two teammates about whom I've been thinking a lot today. A Test debut is a special occasion for any player, let alone one who is 31 years of age, and knowing how hard George Bailey has worked and how much he's achieved in the last couple of years, I am really excited for him. George is a terrific bloke and deserves this.

I have also sat back today and thought a lot about Brad Haddin, who is playing his 50th Test match here. I couldn't be prouder. Hadds is a wonderful fellow, and it's so great to see him back playing for Australia. Twelve months ago, cricket was the last thing on his mind and he probably thought his Test career was over. He has wonderful family and friends who have helped him through that worrying period when his daughter Mia was ill, and also helped him refocus on his ambition to get back into the Australian team. After all that, to see him play his 50th Test match, more matches than all but a small handful of Australian wicketkeepers, is extremely rewarding. I would love nothing more than to win this Test match for my mate Hadds.

So tonight, getting ready for bed, it feels like Christmas Eve. The spirit and feeling amongst the group is great. I can't remember in my career having experienced a team atmosphere so happy, relaxed and excited.

Let's hope Santa brings us what we have asked for.

2

THE FIRST
TEST MATCH

Thursday 21 November. Brisbane.

Whatever you thought about the result, nobody who saw the Ashes series in England this year could have said it wasn't interesting. And today shows that we're in for more of the same in Australia. Interesting cricket, to say the least!

The day dawned warm and fine, and we were in a great mood as we travelled from Southbank to the Gabba. When we got there, I noticed that the wicket was drier than yesterday, definitely a bat-first deck if I won the toss. I expected that there would be a bit of lateral movement before lunch, as usual, but if we could get through the first session unscathed the pitch looked like it would flatten out and offer plenty of runs.

Alastair Cook and I walked out to toss a commemorative coin. He called heads, and it came up tails. At the pitch-side interview, I didn't have much to say, other than to express my feelings in brief: 'Let's go!' We've been waiting for this day, not for a long time in the usual context of Ashes series, but with the utmost keenness.

Mark Taylor presented George Bailey with his cap, a proud moment for all. Mark made a nice speech, saying George deserved to be here and his only advice was for George to continue playing the way he always does. It helped that Mark has been around the group all week, as he's a terrifically bright, positive influence.

We have all noticed and commented on the incredible buzz around Brisbane this week, and this morning it was palpable. After nine straight Test matches in India and England, we have been hungry to play at home. And from the sound of it, the Australian crowds have been just as hungry to see us. We felt it when we lined up for 'Advance Australia Fair', and our team linked arms while we sang. I'm not aware of the boys having done this before. It just happened spontaneously, in response to how united we are feeling and how we can sense the Brisbane crowd's desire to see us do well. It was really special.

After the national anthems, I went to the viewing area of our changing room to watch Chris Rogers and David Warner start the innings. James Anderson took the first over from the Vulture Street end, and as expected there was some sideways movement and a lot more bounce than we've experienced all year, in Test cricket at least.

Davey looked in tremendous touch, always looking for the opportunity to score runs. Stuart Broad's first ball, from the Stanley Street end, was a no-ball bouncer which Davey hooked for four. Next over, Davey cover drove his first ball from Anderson to the boundary. He looked fantastic.

Broad's sharp bounce undid Chris soon after, but the fall of a wicket didn't slow Davey, who hit two fours off Broad in successive balls, a leg glance and another cover drive. When Broad bowled a bouncer next over, Davey upper-cut him over slips for another boundary. The outfield was lush and quite slow, but that didn't stop Davey from hitting six fours off the opening spells from Broad and Anderson.

Chris Tremlett, one of the tallest and biggest bowlers I have ever seen, replaced Anderson in the ninth over, and Shane Watson, who hadn't played any cricket since the last one-dayer in India three weeks ago, was very sound in defence. It's important to put defence first, as we have been saying all year, and I liked the way Watto was building his game from the ground up.

Graeme Swann came into the series in the 18th over from the Stanley Street end, and Davey immediately went down the wicket and on the attack, driving to cover and then lofting one over mid-off.

Things were looking good until about 15 minutes before lunch, when the umpires had a long look at the ball before changing it. I don't know if it was an effect of the different ball, but Broad and Swann bowled better in that last little session with the replacement, and four minutes before the break Broad got one to lift on Watto, drawing the edge to second slip.

So I was in, two minutes before the break. Broad, who had been copping some stick from the crowd and the local newspaper, was bowling very well. They set catchers close in on the leg-side, both in front of and behind square. It was a bouncer field, and Broad's first ball was the opposite – full and straight. I faced a couple more balls, but they were also on a good length, no bouncers before lunch, which we took at 2/71, not a bad start.

It was obvious that England were going to attack me with the short ball. Broad had done it throughout the winter series, and while I don't think I did too badly, it's clear that they think there's a chink there. I've been working hard on it at the National Cricket Centre and at home in Sydney. Aside from getting my back and hamstrings right, so I have maximum flexibility, I have been practising against the short ball by getting Duncan Kerr, my personal trainer, to put a bowling machine up on boxes so it releases the ball from more than seven feet high. We have used tennis balls to exaggerate the bounce, and turned the speed of the machine up as fast as it will go.

The change I have made, technically, is to go back to the preliminary move I had when I was a youngster. Then, my first move as the ball was released was to go back and across with my right foot. When I started to play senior cricket, I changed that preliminary move to a half-step forward with my left foot, to counter the pitched-up ball aiming for a slips catch or an LBW. Last year, when the South African bowlers were using their bouncers and bowling short at me on Australian wickets, I worked out a plan to revert to the back and across at the start of my innings against certain bowlers, such as Morne Morkel.

In the past five or six weeks, I have been working on that as my triggering move for some bowlers, such as Broad, early in my innings: the back and across rather than the half-step forward.

When we came out after lunch, Swann was bowling and I got off the mark with a single. This put me on strike to Broad next over. He bowled three full-pitched balls, which I defended, and then the short one. Maybe it was the pressure of the moment, but for some reason I abandoned the plan I had been working on for more than a month, and reverted to what was comfortable: the half-step forward. Broad got the next ball to bounce up at my chest, and I was out of position, too far forward, and was only able to fend it to short leg.

Of course I was disappointed at getting out, but the reason I was really mad at myself was my mental process.

I had made a plan, a good plan, and then out in the middle I had not kept faith with it. Going back and across to that ball, I'm sure I would have dealt with it. Going forward, I was right out of position. I was angry about not having trusted myself.

I also knew that my dismissal would add to the English team's theory, and possibly a public perception, that I have a problem with the short ball. They will be telling themselves they have me under pressure with this tactic.

Honestly, I don't think I have a problem with the short ball. When I was playing South Africa last summer, Morkel, Dale Steyn and Vernon Philander bowled a lot of short balls at me and I made two double-centuries. I look at the short ball as an opportunity to score runs. It has got me out a few times, sure, but people say I'm a good player of spin bowling and I've got out a lot of times to spinners, too. People may have an opinion about me and the short ball, and bowlers may have an opinion, but the only place where it counts is in my head. Today I let myself down in the heat of the moment. At the same time, you've got to give credit where it's due. Broad bowled well all day, and he got that ball right where he wanted it.

We had a bit of a setback in that post-lunch period. Davey was 49 and looking set for a big score when he got caught at cover, George missed out on debut, and Steve Smith was working his way nicely towards a significant innings when he was another to be caught close to the wicket off a rising delivery from Tremlett. We were 6/132 when Mitchell Johnson went out to join Brad Haddin, and I'm sure there were people who were thinking, 'Here we go again.' The Australian top order does not have a pretty record over the past two series. But I am absolutely certain that we have a new strength and solidity in this team that has come from the dark experiences we have undergone this year. We've learnt more and more about how to deal with pressure situations, we've talked about it at length, and we know what to do. It is just a matter of putting our words into action.

Under pressure, Hadds's approach is to not let himself go tight. Early in his innings, he likes to play his shots, and that's what he did today, hitting a beautiful pull shot off Anderson over the fence, which I think was his first boundary. Mitch is also a free-flowing batsman when his mind is clear, and it was thoroughly enjoyable to watch the pair of them pull us out of the position we were in, not only for the result they achieved this afternoon but for the counter-attacking brand of cricket they played. I am really hoping that the confidence Mitch will have derived from his innings will flow through into his bowling. His past career suggests this is the case, with a strong positive relationship between his batting and his bowling.

We lost Mitch late in the day to a good Broad in-swinger, but he and Hadds got us into what I think is a fifty-fifty position in the match. We would have liked to lose fewer wickets, but the outfield is slow and if we can get around or above 300, that might be a better score than some observers think. You never know how good a score is until both teams have batted. I think this wicket will offer something to our fast bowlers.

Runs tomorrow morning will be crucial. Hadds is in the seventies, and I'll say a prayer tonight that he goes on to make a hundred. It has already been a special innings by a special player. I hoped the cricket gods would look after him at Trent Bridge in July. They didn't, so I hope they figure they owe him one now.

Friday 22 November. Brisbane.

What an amazing day. I don't think I've had a better day since taking over the captaincy two years ago. Everything went to plan.

Except, maybe, for Hadds not getting a hundred. He certainly deserved one. But he lost Ryan Harris early so Hadds, as he always does, decided to take more risks than usual in the hope of scoring quick runs for the team. Batting with Nathan Lyon, he was on 94 when he tried to come back for an impossible second run, and got run out. I don't know how many times I have said it before, but it sets a fantastic example to all the players when they see the vice-captain prepared to sacrifice himself for the team cause.

With almost 300 runs on the board, we went out into the field full of enthusiasm but also knowing that we had to bowl and field at our best to contain England. We were confident, but by no means over-confident. Initially, Ryan Harris and Mitchell Johnson bowled very fast – I think their first two overs contained the fastest 12 balls so far in the match – and the brand-new ball was swinging, but we didn't control it well enough to make Alastair Cook and Michael Carberry play as much as we would have liked. The English left-handers are both keen to leave as many balls as possible, and we played into their hands a little.

I brought Sidds on from the Vulture Street end to settle things down and apply a bit more scoreboard pressure. He did just that, and helped Rhino get the wicket at the other end: a well-pitched-up ball outside off stump that Cook nicked. It was the same way we got him out repeatedly in England, frustrating him into playing at a ball he might have preferred to leave.

Jonathan Trott came in, and it was no secret that we were going to target him with the short ball. During the winter Ashes series, after a positive start, he'd seemed to lose some confidence, and by the time of the one-dayers he was getting into some awkward positions when Mitch in particular was directing the ball into his ribs.

I brought Mitch back on, but as luck would have it, he bowled two overs exclusively at Carberry. We were talking a lot in the cordon about where to place a catcher behind the wicket on the leg-side, a fine leg slip or a wider man at leg gully. It's a fine line. Obviously you always set a field for where you think you can get a certain batsman out, but you don't want to set a field for a bad ball. At the end of the day, you're thinking about how to complement your bowlers. While Carberry and Trott were together, we moved the men around, in and out of the leg-side catching positions, but it didn't quite work: Carberry tickled one fine at catchable height off Mitch, but not when we had a fielder there, and when he put one in the air squarer, the fielder was too fine.

It was this kind of ball, however, short and into the body, that got Trott out just before lunch. In the third over of his new spell, Mitch finally had Trott on strike. With his distinctive forward movement, Trott was wanting to get across inside the line and hit the ball to the on-side. He did it with a few, but put them in the air, not quite controlled.

Sidds had what looked like the last over before lunch, but he rushed through the final couple of balls to give Mitch a chance to bowl another, going into the 'red zone' in terms of time, with Trott on strike. I moved Nathan Lyon to deep square leg, the position where Usman Khawaja had caught Trott with a sort of shovel-pull stroke he plays off his hip to the rising ball. With the man out there, I thought it might put some doubt in Trott's mind about whether he could play that shot and get away with it. Mitch bowled one in that area, right on his hip, and Trott got too far inside the line, possibly wanting to hit it fine of the square leg fielder, and flicked at it.

When Hadds took the catch, all the boys went up except me. I didn't think Trott had hit it. I didn't hear a thing! But the umpire's finger went up. I looked at Trott, and thought he was going to ask the umpire to go to the Decision Referral System (DRS), getting the opinion of the video umpire. But no, Trott walked off; we had him. It was a great way to go into the lunch break: to have squeezed in that extra over, to have worked out the right plan for Trott, and to have executed it. It was also Hadds's 200th Test catch, a nice way to ice the cake for him. The only thing missing was the captain's hearing!

After lunch, Kevin Pietersen looked in ominous form. This is his hundredth Test match, and he's the type of guy who will characteristically lift himself for the big occasion. He can be a sketchy starter, but he wasn't today. I had Sidds and Rhino bowling together, to keep things tight rather than feed Pietersen's aggression. In Sidds's eighth over, Pietersen hit a drive at catchable height back down the wicket. It didn't come quite as hard as Sidds expected, and he dropped it. By no means was it a simple chance, but England were 2/70, Pietersen was 8, and I was desperately hoping we would not live to regret it.

Sidds and Rhino bowled an impressive containing spell, and then I brought Nathan Lyon on. Immediately he had the ball turning and jumping away from the left-handed Carberry. That was encouraging. I loved the way the bowlers were working together, in pairs. Sidds and Rhino, alternating from the Vulture Street end, tied Pietersen down in order to frustrate him and to keep the left-hander, Carberry, on strike to Nathan. They built up the pressure, until, with his sixth ball in his new spell, Rhino had Pietersen falling across a little to the off-side and he clipped a catch to George Bailey at mid-wicket. That was a big one.

Ian Bell was the guy we couldn't formulate an effective plan for in England. We have tried to develop a few new ideas for him now. I brought Mitch on to replace Rhino, and he seemed to find a better control of his line and length from the Vulture Street end with a slightly older ball. He switched to bowling around the wicket at Carberry, an unusual angle. With Mitch's low arm, the ball would have been coming from a place a left-hander like Carberry can't have seen much of before. We figured out that Carberry was quite structured in his approach, and was comfortable leaving the ball a lot when it came from a left-armer or a right-armer bowling over the wicket. We just thought the left-arm around the wicket angle was going to force him to play at the ball more often than he was comfortable doing.

Mitch bowled as good a three-ball sequence as you could see on a cricket field. His first ball was a snorter, which Carberry, who had looked quite safe for two and a half hours, was only able to parry just square of the short leg fieldsman. Next ball was a higher bouncer. Carberry, who had been leaving everything he could, suddenly went for a hook shot, and missed it. The third ball was slanting across him on a good length, pitching middle, going away, and he went to play at it. As he changed his mind and tried to pull his bat away, he outside-edged the ball. Watto pocketed it at first slip, and we were over the moon.

Our spirits were up now, as we could feel the momentum shift. England were 4/87, and vulnerable. Nathan was getting some nice bounce out of the wicket. Next over, he dismissed Bell and Matt Prior almost identically from successive balls that jumped, took the inside edge, and were caught at short leg by Steve Smith. On the dismissal of Prior, neither Nathan nor the umpire, Aleem Dar, heard or saw the nick. Smithy and Hadds were adamant, and I called for the referral, which showed a clear contact between bat and ball.

This put Nathan on a hat-trick, and although he bowled a good ball first-up to Stuart Broad, he didn't get the wicket. But his two dismissals in an over, making it three in five minutes, had us flying. Joe Root was caught edging into the slips cordon, and Mitch had Graeme Swann caught at bat-pad off another inside edge. At tea England were 8/94, an amazing transformation. They had lost six wickets for nine runs, starting with the Pietersen dismissal. For the first time this year, we had set off a major collapse. It felt good for the boot to be on our foot for once.

After tea, the floodlights were turned on to counter some gathering clouds, but there was no rain forecast. Rhino and Mitch sustained a short-pitched attack at Broad and Tremlett, very tall men who have trouble getting out of the way. The rules stipulate no more than two balls an over rising above the shoulders, and one of the advantages of such tall batsmen is that it's hard to get the ball going that high. Most of the bouncers were going into the awkward rib cage and armpit area rather than sailing harmlessly overhead.

Rhino got Tremlett, to a good catch at leg gully taken by Nathan Lyon diving forward, before Broad counter-attacked. We had to finish the job off. England's tail had too often added irritating extra runs during the winter. I brought back Nathan and Peter Siddle in a double change, and eventually Broad top-edged a pull shot off Sidds, which Chris Rogers judged well to catch at deep mid-wicket. England were all out for 136, in four hours. All of a sudden our first innings 295 looked like a very healthy score indeed.

But as we know, the bowling group's good work can be undone very quickly by a substandard production from the batsmen. Once you get momentum, through dismissing the opposition for a low score, you have to keep hold of it, or else you will soon be in trouble again. Very often teams lose wickets late in the day in these circumstances. That's why I was particularly pleased with the way Davey and Chris set about their work. Davey started with a blazing back-foot cover drive off Anderson, and that set the tone. In failing light, for those two to add 65 runs and survive until stumps was almost as good for our morale as what the team had done in the field.

Right now, I can't keep the smile off my face. We haven't won the Test and are not even thinking about the series, but to have a day like today is a fantastic reward for all the work the guys have put in already. There are a lot of things that still have to go our way before we can claim a win, but as an individual day, throughout my career, I can't think of many that have been better than this.

Saturday 23 November. Brisbane.

Today has been another good day from the boys. We know we have a lot of work still to do, but to build a big lead and have England two wickets down, we feel that we are the team with the destiny of this match in our hands.

The day didn't start so well. Chris Rogers and Shane Watson were out in the first half hour, both to shots that showed there was plenty of life in the pitch on this third day. If there is such a thing as encouraging ways to lose wickets, these were just so: I am sure our fast bowlers were quietly pleased to see Stuart Broad and Chris Tremlett getting a lot of bounce still.

When I came in, I was urging myself to stick to the plan I had abandoned in the first innings. I got off the mark from my first ball with a push off the back foot for two, which is always a nice feeling. Then Tremlett bowled a bouncer which sailed high overhead. There was no disguise in England's usual plan. Tremlett had dismissed Watto in his first over, but immediately Alastair Cook told Broad to warm up to bowl at me. I had to face a couple of balls from Anderson, and for the last delivery of the over they dropped the field right back to gift me a single and put me on strike to Broad. Anderson seemed to think this was quite amusing, but it didn't bother me. It would give me the chance to face a lot of balls early, which I like. Sometimes you can be in for five overs and not face a ball, and you get a bit anxious, wanting the feeling of bat on ball. So it didn't faze me to have to face Broad when I was fresh; in fact I preferred it.

Broad started, as he had in the first innings, with three fullish balls, all of which I had to defend. His first bouncer was the fourth ball of the over. I had been saying, in my head, *Back yourself and play the way you play best*. I stuck to the plan of moving my right foot back and across, and I just saw the ball and reacted to it, freeing myself up and not worrying about the possibility of getting out. It all sounds so easy afterwards, but at the time, it was a matter of trust. Trust the preparation. Trust the plan. Trust that you have done this many times before.

That first bouncer from Broad was over the height of my shoulder and outside the line of the off stump. I was able to pull it down in front of square leg, and timed it well enough to get it away for four. Things just felt right; it's a mystery of cricket, how on a given day that feeling is there. Broad's next ball was another bouncer, but not as high, and was angled slightly down the leg-side. I got inside it and hooked it very fine for another four. His last ball in that over was shortish, not a bouncer, on the line of off stump, and I pushed a single through cover. It was as if everything turned around in that over, and the doubts about me and the short ball, whoever held them, had gone away. For today, at least.

But there is always a new challenge. A few minutes later, rain began to fall while I was facing Anderson. Not wanting too much rain to get on the wicket, the umpires took us off at the end of the over and we would have to start again.

The delay was only ten minutes or so, and my concentration was unimpaired when we came back out. It certainly helped to be batting with Davey at his brilliant best. We saw off Anderson and Broad, and Swann bowled pretty well until the lunch break. But by then we were 2/145, a lead of about 300, and were feeling that we had stabilised things after those early wickets. We scored ten runs off Swann's first over after lunch, and he was taken off. Joe Root bowled some off-spin from the other end, and we found we had enough opportunities to score off him too.

Davey clubbed Anderson over mid-off for four, and was on a roll. It was only when he got close to his hundred that Anderson had him playing and missing a couple of times. At that point, Anderson bowled his best over of the day. I did my best to get Davey to three figures by taking a single off Root, and Davey brought up his century with a drive through a packed off-side field.

He was pumped, of course. It was his first Test century since Adelaide last year, when he hit the South Africans around the park. I couldn't be prouder of the way he has come back from a tumultuous first half of the year, and I was thrilled to be out there with him at this significant moment in his career. It is a reminder that the work David has been putting in, on and off the field, produces results.

Swann was brought back on at the Vulture Street end, and we scored 28 off his two overs before he was taken off again. There was no set plan to take him on. You can't bat against such a good bowler with a preconceived idea of hitting him out of the attack. But generally facing a spinner at the Gabba is easier than elsewhere. There is consistent bounce and not a lot of spin. So we saw an opportunity to play with positive intent, rotate the strike, back ourselves, play the way Davey and I usually do when we're in together. Today, it worked.

I felt comfortable throughout the afternoon. You can't depend on scoring runs against good bowlers without a bit of luck on your side, however, and I had that when I curled an inside-edged on-drive just wide of Swann at mid-wicket, then chopped one from Broad just past my stumps. But aside from the odd mishap, I felt I was moving my feet quickly and seeing the ball well. It was a relief that when England's short-pitched attack didn't work, they didn't seem to have another set plan of attack, or if they did, they couldn't get it working.

Davey and I got our partnership past the 150 mark, at better than five runs an over, until the last over before drinks in the middle session. He smacked Broad back over his head for a dead-straight six, but nicked one later that over. It was just a fantastic, exhilarating innings, and I had the best seat in the house.

Smithy came and went, but it was lovely to spend some quality time in the middle with George Bailey, who was much more settled after getting his first Test innings out of the way two days ago. Anderson came on for a short spell before being replaced by Swann, and Root was brought back, but George and I were going along at a good clip, building the lead. George got Root away for a handsome six over mid-on, which must surely have calmed the nerves. I can still remember my Test debut clearly – what I can't remember is how I got any runs, I was so hyped-up. But George is a lot more mature than I was on debut.

After a bit of a lull, I got Root away on the on-side to bring up a hundred, which was nice personally, not the score as such but to have played some attacking cricket and to have countered England's plans. I have still got some work to do to get my game to where I want it to be, but this was a settling innings. When you get runs early in a series, you feel like you have got the monkey off your back. On 113 I threw my wicket away, charging at Swann, and while I always want to get more runs I wasn't overly annoyed. We were in a position now where we were dictating the course of the match and I could start thinking about a declaration.

After George was bowled by Swann, Hadds and Mitch put the team first yet again and batted with enterprise and aggression. When he got to his second 50 of his 50th Test match, Hadds shot a glance towards the changing room to see if I wanted them to come in. But I wasn't thinking about the runs as such. Once our lead had passed 500, I knew we had more than enough runs on the board. The question facing me was how many overs I wanted our boys to bowl this evening. Around 15 overs would give the bowlers one good spell each, and leave the ball still new enough tomorrow morning. I declared when we reached that point, basing the declaration on overs more than runs.

We were really fired up when we went into the field. It's a great sense you get in the team, when you have a big lead and you can put every last ounce of your energy into a short session at the end of the day's play. You know the batsmen are thinking of nothing but survival, so the cricket is most likely going to be played on your terms.

Ryan Harris bowled a good full length to Cook, just where we wanted it, but it was Carberry he got first. He pushed the left-hander back, Carberry played it down defensively, and the ball ran back onto the stumps between his legs, a little unluckily for him.

Our plan against Trott was simple, and he was trying to counteract it in a similar fashion to how he'd attempted it yesterday, by getting inside the line of the ball and playing his horizontal-bat shots. He hit one up in the air which fell into space, but then, against Mitch, he played that same half-pull off his hip and the high ball was well taken by Nathan Lyon, in the same deep square leg position that I was now customarily setting against Trott.

Kevin Pietersen was, as usual, keen to get off the mark, and we nearly had a third wicket when he called Cook for a precarious single. Unfortunately George Bailey knocked off a bail before taking the ball, and Cook survived. But the bowlers kept charging in, and were a constant threat until the last ball.

Cook and Pietersen are still there tonight – they're both champions with around 8000 Test match runs in their careers and they will make sure we have to fight for wickets tomorrow. We have a lot of work to do. These two days in a row have been fantastic for us, but they will count for nothing if we can't finish the job.

Sunday 24 November. **Brisbane.**

Well, it's been a long time between team songs. What is it, ten Test matches since we beat Sri Lanka at the SCG last January? It feels like a lot longer. I can promise you, we are going to enjoy every minute of it – and then reset ourselves to do it again.

It has also been a heated, controversial day, at the end anyway. But I'll get to that. The controversies do not add up to much beside what was a truly great Test match victory for Australia.

We have had a mantra throughout this match of 'Every run counts'. During breaks, even between overs, the boys have been calling out to each other, 'Come on, every run counts!' That may sound a bit odd when we have won a match by nearly 400 runs. But we have set ourselves to play our Test cricket with this level of intensity. Every run does count! In England, at Nottingham, we had this lesson confirmed the hard way. We lost a five-day match by 14 runs. Every run counts, right down to the last one. And that is going to be the way we play right through to the last ball of the last Test match in Sydney in January. If England don't understand how intensely and with how much hunger we are playing our cricket, they will by the end of the summer.

Today was very humid, promising a solid test for bowlers and batsmen alike. I started with Peter Siddle from the Vulture Street end and Ryan Harris from the Stanley Street end, with the aim of making Cook and Pietersen know that this was going to be a hard day for them, ball after ball of intense pressure. If they were going to set up a match-saving partnership, good luck to them, but we wanted them to know that none of it was going to be easy.

Sidds started a really good spell with some beautiful rhythm first-up. He didn't take a wicket, but beat Pietersen so often, just catching the inside edge a couple of times, that Kevin must have known he was going to have to work his backside off for every run. Cook also nicked one, but it failed to carry to second slip. Sidds also had Pietersen playing and missing outside the off stump. Our aim was to create chances, and even though the wickets were not falling initially, we trusted that if we kept creating those chances the results would come.

With Cook, we kept pitching it up on the off-side. His strength square of the wicket, cutting and pulling, is well established. He loves the ball on his pads or on his hip. Some of us have strong and not particularly happy memories of him scoring more than 700 runs and batting for day after day in the last Ashes series here, in 2010–11. He is such a good player, we said in our meetings that if he is going to make a hundred, let's make him score his runs in places where he's not used to scoring them, for example driving on the off-side through mid–off or extra-cover. To achieve this, you have to bowl in certain places, but also have the right field settings. At one point I set a field for Cook with nobody in front of point on the off-side except for an unorthodox short mid-off, which we call 'man on the wicket'. The fieldsman is not actually on the wicket, of course, but he is close to the strip and most of the way to the bowler's end, sort of like a deep silly mid-off. I don't know how many balls the fielder stopped, but it is a way of forcing a batsman out of his comfort zone and keeping him thinking.

Fairly early in the first session, I brought on Nathan Lyon and Mitchell Johnson, not wanting to wear out any of the bowlers with long spells. But Cook and Pietersen dug in, and got to the first drinks break at 2/71, no doubt gaining confidence from every little milestone they survived.

It was straight after the drinks break that we got our man. Mitch bowled his first short ball to Pietersen, and it didn't really get up. Pietersen top-edged his hook shot. Who was under it at fine leg? Ryan Harris, who has just about the safest pair of hands in the country? No – Ryan was off the field after drinks, taking a toilet break. The man under the ball was Chris Sabburg, a Queensland club cricketer who has had a bit of first-class and State limited-overs experience. Darren Lehmann knows Chris from his days coaching the Bulls and the Brisbane Heat, and Chris was one of three players Boof had drafted in to help us out as reserve fielders. We had no access to Queensland's active Sheffield Shield players, because they are involved in a match interstate. It must be a pretty daunting experience for these young club cricketers, going into the Australian team changing room and onto the field in a Test match, but I have to say they have all been absolutely fantastic throughout this game. Chris Sabburg took the catch safely, and we mobbed him. And then he was straight off again, as Rhino was ready to come back on.

Mitch got fired up after taking Pietersen's wicket, and rattled Ian Bell with some short ones. Cook might have been thrown out of his usually unflappable calm, because he missed a full toss from Nathan Lyon that, unluckily for us, wasn't going to hit the stumps. Mitch came around the wicket at Cook for a short period, and then Sidds came on and nearly bowled Cook with one that deviated down off the bottom of the thigh pad.

Just before lunch, I tried a few different things. Smithy had a bowl, just to see if he could come up with something, and Shane Watson replaced Sidds. Watto very nearly got Cook, with a checked drive that went in the air down the pitch but landed centimetres in front of Watto's boots.

After lunch, we started with Mitch and Rhino, and the whole team came out with plenty of energy. It was a willing period, with everyone knowing how important it was to break the Bell–Cook partnership, and of course the English pair would have known how important it was to stay together. Cook cut Mitch for a couple of fours, but as soon as Rhino switched to bowling around the wicket he beat the left-hander's edge. Mitch charged in at Bell and delivered some fierce bouncers that nearly bent the batsman double as he swayed back out of the ball's path.

As per the weather forecast, the clouds were beginning to gather. Kevin Mitchell and his staff, every bit as ominous as a storm front, were clustering together on the side of the ground with their tractors and covers. The atmosphere seemed to be thickening around us, the way it does in Brisbane before a big storm. It feels electric, literally. A fired-up Sidds got a ball to follow Bell's bat as he tried to pull it away, and Hadds took the catch. Funnily, just like me with the Trott dismissal in the first innings, Watto hadn't heard a thing and didn't appeal. This time I saw the deflection. We were exuberant.

About 15 minutes later, the lights had come on and the thunder was getting closer, and just after I brought Mitch back on for Sidds we were taken from the field.

The rain was incredible. It pelted down, and soon turned into hail. Within a few minutes, the Gabba had turned as white as if it was snowing. We detected that the English players, in the viewing room next to ours, were very happy, but we were confident we would be back on soon. This month, on a lot of the days since I have been up in Brisbane, there have been late afternoon and evening thunderstorms. They are heavy, but they're also short. They just blow over. The Gabba is a well-drained ground, and even though the water was now pooling on the grass as the hail melted, I knew how quickly it could be ready again for play.

We all did our own thing during the break. Some boys had treatment with the physio, some had ice baths, and some sat talking about the game. We were all ultra-keen to get back on the field. Sure enough, the sun was soon shining and the ground staff were at work with their drying equipment, and in the end we were off the field for 92 minutes, which, including the tea break, meant we had only lost a little more than an hour from the match. Incredible. If you saw the hail on the ground, you could be forgiven for thinking any more cricket today was an impossibility.

Our whole team kept reminding each other that every run was valuable and we had to work to create our chances. Mitch started up from the Vulture Street end to Joe Root, and put in some short ones that whizzed by and thumped into Hadds's gloves.

It was at the other end that the damage was done. Nathan Lyon, second ball after the break, bowled one to Cook that was a fraction short of a length. Cook went back to cut it, and it turned and hopped enough to get the edge. Hadds, impeccable as ever, took what is always a difficult chance, the deflection off a spin bowler, and we had the England captain, the man who is such a threat to bat for a long, long time.

With Cook out and the thunder and lightning behind us, we were on a roll again. Momentum is hard to grab, but we are learning that once we have it, we have to run with it and not let it go. In Nathan's next over, we set Davey Warner at leg slip. Matt Prior hasn't been in the best form, and we figured that he would be pretty keen to get bat on ball. Nathan bowled one turning down leg, and Prior reached forward and tickled it around the corner, straight to Davey.

Mitch was ready to capitalise. His first ball to Stuart Broad, the new batsman, was from around the wicket, and it reared into his armpit. Broad gloved it, giving another catch off the rising fast ball. Minutes later, Graeme Swann, who has a record of stubborn resistance at the bottom of the order, edged Mitch to third slip, where Smithy took a sharp chance. It says a lot about the quality of the wicket that edges were still carrying to third slip late on day four of the Test match.

We had now taken four wickets for nine runs in a bit over three overs. It was reminiscent of the first innings. In the afternoon, with a sultry atmosphere, the Gabba can feel like a dangerous place to bat.

Another storm was looking like it might close in, and we were keen to create another chance. Another two, and we would win the Test match. When the next storm came, we had to stop playing again, but the system skirted Woolloongabba and we were only off for 15 or so minutes.

Back on the field, we referred an appeal against Chris Tremlett to DRS, but the catch had come off his arm guard. I brought Rhino on to replace Mitch from the Vulture Street end, after a five-over spell in which Mitch had taken two wickets for four runs. Rhino then set up Tremlett well with some short balls, eventually getting the catch popped to short leg.

Anderson was the last man in. Meanwhile, Joe Root had watched all the carnage from the non-striker's end, a good place to bat in these conditions. We thought we had the match done and dusted when the batsmen got mixed up and Root was well out of his ground, apparently run out. But Nathan Lyon, who had broken the wicket, wasn't celebrating, and it was soon clear that he had dislodged a bail prematurely with his hand. We stalled the celebration. I kept saying to the boys, 'Let's create another chance!'

It was just after that, when the game should have been over anyway, that Anderson and George Bailey, who was in a helmet at short leg, began talking to each other. It was clear from Anderson's body language that some kind of confrontation was taking place, and I went to stand up for George. I thought, the guy is playing his first Test match, he doesn't need to be stood over or threatened by a veteran like Anderson.

I went forward to tell Anderson to get on with the game, and as I walked away from him, I said, 'Get ready for a broken f---ing arm.'

I said it because I was angry at the way he had been speaking to George. I was only sticking up for my teammate. But I acknowledge that my language was unacceptable, and it was picked up by the stump microphone and broadcast by Channel Nine. When we came off the field, I was unaware that this was the case. I was informed about the broadcast of my words only in the press conference after the match. I know there are young boys and girls watching, as well as adults who would be offended by my language. I would never wish bad things to happen to anybody, and I certainly didn't want James Anderson to get injured. I was sticking up for a teammate, but my language was provocative. I think what happens on the field should stay on the field, and everybody shook hands extremely respectfully at the end of the match, when, a few balls later, Anderson popped one in the air and Mitch took his ninth wicket.

We were ecstatic. Winning is a great feeling, all the more so when it has been a little while coming. After we shook hands with the English players, we went to our changing room where Nathan Lyon got to lead the team victory song, 'Underneath the Southern Cross I Stand', for the first time since he inherited the role from Mike Hussey last January. Nathan stood in the centre of the group and did his best to get through the unfamiliar rituals of calling out highlights from the game, and we loved hearing it. He has a distinctive singing voice and we joined in with him. It was an emotional moment for all of us.

Mitchell Johnson was presented with the gold blazer for man of the match, a recognition of the journey he has taken to get back into the team and to be at his very best. We are all extremely proud of him, and glad he is on our side!

I knew we had it in us, but I guess we had yet to prove it until today. You can talk all you like about confidence, but you don't know for sure that you can win a match like this until you have actually done it. Now we had, and it means a great deal to us. I hope it creates a psychological effect in the England changing room too. Surely now they know what we can do.

After the match, I had to go and do my press conference, Mitch coming with me as the official man of the match. It was there that I first heard that the stump mike had picked up my comment to Anderson. I was taken aback, but I don't blame the microphone, I blame myself. I told the journalists, 'There's always banter on the field between Australia and England. I feel there's a good mutual respect between the teams. You don't get to number one in the world, as they have done, without playing successful cricket over a long period. The banter's no different from what it's been throughout my career.'

When they pressed me on what I said personally to Anderson, I was a little unprepared, but I could do nothing but speak honestly. 'Nothing went beyond what I've heard through my career. I cop as much as I give, that's for sure. What is said on the field is part and parcel of the game. We respect the England team as players. Both teams want to win so badly. We all respect the traditions of the game. Ashes cricket has always been competitive. I don't think the line has been crossed. Banter goes both ways. There are plenty of things you don't hear on stump mike that are meant to stay on the field. There are no personal vendettas and no disrespect.'

Verbal exchanges on a cricket field are all part of a player's search to get the best out of himself. In my view, from what I've observed through my career, the verbal side of cricket has far more to do with oneself than it has with the opponent. There are plenty of cricketers at every level who do not say anything at all to their opponents. There are others who love getting involved. Our team has a mix of both types, and I know there are several in the English team who are just the same. You are working on yourself, not the opposition. The players understand that, and there it stops.

Aside from addressing that, I did my best to keep the focus on the real news, which was that we had beaten England in an Ashes Test match for the first time in three years. A lot of hard work went into this over a long period of time, not just this week, but throughout the winter tour. We took confidence out of the back half of the England series, and out of the one-dayers in England and in India. Everybody in our squad is a better player now than they were back in July.

Being back at home, we are all feeling more confident in these conditions, and that's a real positive for us. The support from the Brisbane people has been magnificent. I get that kind of support from family and close friends every match, but the way we got it from that crowd at the Gabba, it had a State of Origin feeling. I now know how those Queensland rugby league players feel, to have that kind of crowd behind them!

What really excites me at the moment is that I have just played in a Test match that, apart from half of day one, showcased some of the best cricket I have been involved with. Even before the result, we had an exceptional belief that we were ready. I never felt that we were over-confident that we were going to win. I can safely say that after the event, but it's true. We were always focused on what we had to do next.

As a team we have copped a fair bit of criticism during the past year, and our performances deserve that. We have had to overcome the mental challenge of finishing a Test match off, proving to ourselves that we couldn't just dominate a match but *win* it. But the most exciting thing for us as a team is the attacking style of cricket we are playing. It's a satisfying feeling that we have a result to reflect that. If we keep playing this way, we believe we will have more success.

With my media duties finished, I went back to the changing rooms, where we all stayed until about 10.30 pm tonight. We had a lot of parents and friends, even grandparents, come into the changing room after the Test finished. George Bailey's dad was there, lapping up the thrill of a winning Test match on debut.

Now that the celebrations are over, late at night, I have noticed another good sign: the celebrations *are* over. The boys didn't go overboard. We came back to the team hotel and had a quick drink in the bar, and then everyone just got on with life. We all know that another Test match, in Adelaide, is coming. We haven't won anything, just one Test. It won't count if we don't win the Ashes.

Tuesday 26 November. Brisbane.

After one night at home in Sydney, I have come back to Brisbane to start my preparation for the Second Test match. I will follow a lot of the same routines at the National Cricket Centre as I did before the First Test. I brought Duncan Kerr, my personal trainer, with me and we will have plenty of working out and resting to make sure my body is in peak condition. The hot weather will also be a good preparation for Adelaide.

A couple of off-field storms have broken since the end of the Test match. The International Cricket Council match referee fined me 20 per cent of my match fee for my language to James Anderson on Sunday afternoon. I accept the fine without any complaint. I was angry about the way James spoke to George Bailey, but that is no excuse. I'm annoyed at what came out of my mouth. If a kid says the same kind of thing on a cricket field this weekend, and he says he can say it because it's the same thing the Australian captain said in an Ashes Test match, I will feel responsible for that.

The big news is that Jonathan Trott has left the England squad to go home. Their official statement was that he is getting treatment for a long-running stress-related illness. I have friends who have gone through depression. I don't know if that's what Jonathan is dealing with, but whatever it is, I have great sympathy for anyone who is suffering something like that. Jonathan is a part of the cricket fraternity and at these moments we are all brothers. I rang Alastair Cook to let him know, on behalf of all the Australian players, that we wish the best for Jonathan.

Trott's departure has thrown some light back on the comments David Warner made in his press conference after day three of the Test match. He said he thought some of the English batsmen looked scared of our short-pitched bowling attack, particularly Mitchell Johnson. The England squad are not sheeting home Trott's departure to what Davey said, but Alastair said after the match that he didn't think Davey's comments on Trott, where he described his second-innings dismissal as 'weak', were sportsmanlike.

In defence of Davey, I would say that he is just a very honest bloke without the usual filters other people might place over what they say. With David, what you see is what you get. It wasn't a planned strategy for him to go on the attack and make those comments. He said what he thought, nothing more or less. We have plans in batting and bowling, but not in targeting anyone verbally. I had a quiet word with Davey to remind him of the consequences that may arise from his public statements. It will be for him to decide in future how he wants to respond to questions in media conferences. But I don't think I can rightly stand in the way of a strong character who says what he thinks. If David has breached any code of conduct, it is up to the authorities to adjudicate that.

Aside from that, there has been a great feeling around the country following our win in the First Test match. The way we played at the Gabba has ignited public interest in the series, and support for our team. We have had a tough time in losing the past three Ashes series, and Australians love rallying around their boys when we are the underdogs.

For me personally, what is most pleasing is how we set out our plans and stuck to them. The wicket had pace and bounce, which you could use both ways, batting and bowling, to your advantage. Mitch was the headline act for his bowling, but Peter Siddle, Ryan Harris and Nathan Lyon all gave Mitch the freedom to bowl the way he did through their discipline and control. I told them before the Test match that they are the best bowling attack in the world. I truly believe that. But each player has a role to play, he's bowling for the team, and for the guy bowling at the other end. For example, Sidds bowled to keep the left-handers on strike to Nathan. Whoever was bowling with Mitch had to keep it tight. Sometimes Mitch wanted a certain batsman kept on strike, and to do so he needed good work from his teammate bowling at the other end. It all went well. The batsmen have to do a bit more work, myself included, and adapt to different conditions in Adelaide. The fielding and catching in Brisbane were of a pleasingly high standard, showing the benefits of the work we've done with Steve Rixon, Mike Young and Mark Taylor. Our catching was how it has got to be if we are to win this series.

We will play a similar attacking brand of cricket in Adelaide, but we'll have to do it differently. The Adelaide Oval will have a drop-in wicket, grown and prepared elsewhere and transplanted into the oval, for the first time for a Test match, as the ground is being repurposed as an Australian rules football stadium in winter. Judging by the drop-in wickets used so far in the Sheffield Shield, Adelaide's new wicket will not present us with the opportunity to rely on bounce and seam movement. More likely, the pitch will be low and slow and abrasive, and there will be spin and reverse swing, which will bring Anderson and Swann into the game more than in Brisbane. We will have to play with the same attitude, but different tactics.

It would be silly for us to be over-excited by what happened at the Gabba. We've got the result we have been crying out for for a long time, but now we start again. Come Adelaide, there will be no runs on the board, no wickets, and the scorecard will be blank.

I will be settling down in Brisbane from now until Friday, when I fly back to Sydney for a day at home. Then on Sunday it's down to Adelaide to get together with the boys, and it's all on again.

First Test
21–24 November 2013.
Brisbane Cricket Ground, Woolloongabba

Australia (first innings)

Batting		R	B	4	6	SR
CJL Rogers	c: Bell b: Broad	1	9	0	0	11.11
DA Warner	c: Pietersen b: Broad	49	82	6	0	59.75
SR Watson	c: Swann b: Broad	22	71	2	0	30.98
MJ Clarke	c: Bell b: Broad	1	10	0	0	10.00
SPD Smith	c: Cook b: Tremlett	31	59	4	0	52.54
GJ Bailey	c: Cook b: Anderson	3	15	0	0	20.00
BJ Haddin	run out (Carberry/Prior)	94	153	8	1	61.43
MG Johnson	b: Broad	64	134	6	2	47.76
PM Siddle	c: Cook b: Anderson	7	18	1	0	38.88
RJ Harris	c: Prior b: Broad	9	17	0	0	52.94
NM Lyon	not out	1	16	0	0	6.25
Extras (11lb, 1w, 1nb, 0b)		13				
Total 10 Wkts, 97.1 overs		295		3.03 Runs/Over		

Fall of wickets 1-28 (Cook, 10.2 ov), 2-55 (Trott, 17.1 ov), 3-82 (Pietersen, 30.6 ov), 4-87 (Carberry, 36.3 ov), 5-87 (Bell, 37.2 ov), 6-87 (Prior, 37.3 ov), 7-89 (Root, 38.4 ov), 8-91 (Swann, 40.3 ov), 9-110 (Tremlett, 47.2 ov), 10-136 (Broad, 52.4 ov)

Bowling	O	M	R	W	Econ	SR	Extras
JM Anderson	25.1	5	67	2	2.66	75.5	
SCJ Broad	24	3	81	6	3.37	24	(1nb, 1w)
CT Tremlett	19	3	51	1	2.68	114	
GP Swann	26	4	80	0	3.07	–	
JE Root	3	1	5	0	1.66	–	

England (first innings)

Batting		R	B	4	6	SR
AN Cook	c: Haddin b: Harris	13	30	2	0	43.33
MA Carberry	c: Watson b: Johnson	40	113	4	0	35.39
IJL Trott	c: Haddin b: Johnson	10	19	1	0	52.63
KP Pietersen	c: Bailey b: Harris	18	42	1	0	42.85
IR Bell	c: Smith b: Lyon	5	16	0	0	31.25
JE Root	c: Smith b Johnson	2	7	0	0	28.57
MJ Prior	c: Smith b Lyon	0	1	0	0	0.00
SCJ Broad	c: Rogers b: Siddle	32	45	3	0	71.11
GP Swann	c: Bailey b: Johnson	0	5	0	0	0.00
CT Tremlett	c: Lyon b: Harris	8	27	1	0	29.62
JM Anderson	not out	2	10	0	0	20.00
Extras (2lb, 0w, 0nb, 4b)		6				
Total 10 Wkts, 52.4 overs		136		2.58 Runs/Over		

Fall of wickets 1-28 (Cook, 10.2 ov), 2-55 (Trott, 17.1 ov), 3-82 (Pietersen, 30.6 ov), 4-87 (Carberry, 36.3 ov), 5-87 (Bell, 37.2 ov), 6-87 (Prior, 37.3 ov), 7-89 (Root, 38.4 ov), 8-91 (Swann, 40.3 ov), 9-110 (Tremlett, 47.2 ov), 10-136 (Broad, 52.4 ov)

Bowling	O	M	R	W	Econ	SR	Extras
RJ Harris	15	5	28	3	1.86	30	
MG Johnson	17	2	61	4	3.58	25.5	
PM Siddle	11.4	3	24	1	2.05	70	
NM Lyon	9	4	17	2	1.88	27	

Australia (second innings)

Batting		R	B	4	6	SR
CJL Rogers	c: Carberry b: Broad	16	81	1	0	19.75
DA Warner	c: Prior b: Broad	124	154	13	1	80.51
SR Watson	c: Broad b: Tremlett	6	27	1	0	22.22
MJ Clarke	b: Swann	113	130	9	1	86.92
SPD Smith	c: Prior b: Tremlett	0	7	0	0	0.00
GJ Bailey	b: Swann	34	60	1	2	56.66
BJ Haddin	c: Anderson b: Tremlett	53	55	5	0	96.36
MG Johnson	not out	39	45	4	1	86.66
PM Siddle	not out	4	5	1	0	80.00
NM Lyon						
RJ Harris						

Extras	(8lb, 0wb, 0nb, 4b)	12		
Total	7 Wkts, 94 overs	401	4.26 Runs/Over	

Fall of wickets 1-67 (Rogers, 23.1 ov), 2-75 (Watson, 29.3 ov), 3-233 (Warner, 58.4 ov), 4-242 (Smith, 61.4 oh), 5-294 (Clarke, 74.5 ov), 6-305 (Bailey, 78.4 ov), 7-395 (Haddin, 93.1 ov)

Bowling	O	M	R	W	Econ	SR	Extras
JM Anderson	19	2	73	0	3.84	–	
SCJ Broad	16	4	55	2	3.43	48	
CT Tremlett	17	2	69	3	4.05	34	
GP Swann	27	2	135	2	5.00	81	
JE Root	15	2	57	0	3.80		

England (second innings)

Batting		R	B	4	6	SR
AN Cook	c: Haddin b: Lyon	65	195	3	0	33.33
MA Carberry	b: Harris	0	14	0	0	0.00
IJL Trott	c: Lyon b: Johnson	9	9	1	0	100.00
KP Pietersen	c: sub (CJM Sabburg) b: Johnson	26	52	2	0	50.00
IR Bell	c: Haddin b: Siddle	32	70	3	0	45.71
JE Root	not out	26	86	4	0	30.23
MJ Prior	c: Warner b: Lyon	4	8	1	0	50.00
SCJ Broad	c: Haddin b: Johnson	4	3	1	0	133.33
GP Swann	c: Smith b: Johnson	0	2	0	0	0.00
CT Tremlett	c: Bailey b: Harris	7	41	1	0	17.07
JM Anderson	c & b: Johnson	2	8	0	0	25.00

Extras	(2lb, 1w, 1nb, 0b)	4		
Total	10 Wkts, 81.1 overs	179	2.20 Runs/Over	

Fall of wickets 1-1 (Carberry, 4.4 ov), 2-10 (Trott, 7.1 ov), 3-72 (Pietersen, 29.2 ov), 4-130 (Bell, 53.1 ov), 5-142 (Cook, 60.2 ov), 6-146 (Prior, 62.4 ov), 7-151 (Broad, 63.2 ov), 8-151 (Swann, 63.4 ov), 9-172 (Tremlett, 76.5 ov), 10-179 (Anderson, 81.1 ov)

Bowling	O	M	R	W	Econ	SR	Extras
RJ Harris	19	4	49	2	2.57	57	
MG Johnson	21.1	7	42	5	1.98	25.4	(1w)
PM Siddle	15	3	25	1	1.66	90	(1nb)
NM Lyon	20	6	46	2	2.30	60	
SPD Smith	4	1	15	0	3.75	–	
SR Watson	2	2	0	0	0.00	–	

3

THE SECOND TEST MATCH

Sunday 1 December. Adelaide.

We have flown into Adelaide from all over the country, and it's an exciting feeling to see everyone again, even after only a week apart. The selectors have stuck with the same twelve as Brisbane. The Tasmanian guys, George Bailey and James Faulkner, were the last ones to arrive in Adelaide at around eight o'clock tonight. The team has had nothing formal to do, just quick catch-ups in the team hotel and then we have done our own thing for the evening. Most of the boys would have had a good feed, as we will be fasting from midnight tonight until nine o'clock tomorrow morning in order for the medical staff to do some blood tests on us, to check on our wellbeing.

I'm feeling ready to go. My main focus in the early part of this season has been to keep my body as fit and strong as possible in the precious time off that I get between Test matches. As well as the fitness work, ice baths, swimming in the pool, massage and physio I did in Brisbane, I put in plenty of work on my batting too, to replicate my preparation before the First Test match. It's so important, when you are feeling confident in your batting, to score runs and make your form count. The same goes for us as a team: we're flying, but it is imperative that we convert that good feeling into results.

Also, while I was in Brisbane, I watched the England Lions play a local team at the Allan Border Oval. Tim Bresnan hasn't played a first-class match since the Fourth Test match at Durham, when he was an integral part of England's attack and lower-order batting before breaking down with injury. Chris Tremlett didn't take a lot of wickets in Brisbane, so there is a chance Bresnan will come straight in and play in Adelaide. He looks fully fit, and bowled well for the Lions. We have to be ready for all eventualities.

Monday 2 December. Adelaide.

The boys were starving at breakfast! A few of them have big tanks to fill, and were glad we don't have to do this fasting thing very often. At nine o'clock, after the blood tests were done, everyone was hoeing into the food.

After some media commitments in the morning, we trained in the afternoon. Today was the first time I have walked onto the new Adelaide Oval. The new grandstands look amazing, and even though they're not all finished, the existing crowd capacity, of about 30,000, will generate a lot of atmosphere once the game gets going.

The drop-in wicket has caused a lot of speculation. Generally the drop-in wickets used in Sheffield Shield have been difficult for the faster bowlers and friendly to the batsmen. Spinners have taken a high proportion of the wickets, even higher than at the 'old' Adelaide Oval, where spinners tended to do well. I was excited to see what had been prepared, and the pitch has a nice coverage of grass. Some rain is forecast this week, which will keep it from drying out. The ground staff might give it another mow and roll before the Test match starts on Thursday, and it looks like it will have some moisture in it on the first day. All in all, it looks like a good cricket wicket to me, and we are looking forward to testing ourselves out on it.

After a week off, the boys were really switched on with their attitude at training and are looking forward to getting back into it tomorrow. Like me, they have each done their own personal training at home, which is exactly what we require.

The only glitch in a smooth morning was what happened to me. While batting in the second innings of the Test match in Brisbane, I had half-rolled my ankle, and it had been a bit stiff, on and off, since then. When we started running in our warm-up this afternoon, it grabbed a bit. I batted in the nets and practised my slips catching, and felt some discomfort. Afterwards, I put some ice on the ankle. I didn't want to stir it up, but it's a bit sore. It made the evening news, but I am not worried about it. They will have to amputate it to keep me out of the Test match.

Tuesday 3 December. **Adelaide.**

I didn't train today, as a precautionary measure. The physio, Alex Kountouris, and Doc Peter Brukner both advised me not to train after I had two cortisone injections late yesterday. I hate being the subject of speculation, but it is what it is. I'm not in doubt for the Test match, but I suppose if the captain is not training two days out from the first ball of the match, it is bound to cause some comment. The boys in the team are aware that I am going to play, so it doesn't concern them.

It's the first time in a while we have fielded the same team for a second Test match in a row. James Faulkner will be twelfth man again. Everyone knows the team, they are all ready to go, and I can feel the excitement amongst them. As I was unable to bat or field, I went around to individual players for one-on-one chats, making sure they are feeling good about life. I have to say, the way they have trained has been exceptional.

The bowlers have bowled with new balls and also old ones to practise reverse swing, and the batsmen are prepared for an expected England bowling line-up of James Anderson, Stuart Broad, Graeme Swann and either Tim Bresnan or Monty Panesar depending on how their selectors read the pitch.

Our team got just about all of their work in before we were chased off the oval by some dramatic thunderstorms, with lightning and all. I've never experienced that in Adelaide at this time of the year. Normally the weather here for a Test match is hot and sunny, but it looks like being cool and even showery for this one. I know there will be some players who will appreciate that.

Tonight we have a team meeting, our first fines meeting, so that will be fun as long as I don't end up empty-pocketed. The committee usually manage to find some excuse to penalise me for infringements, and there's no higher court to appeal to! I am confident I will be able to train tomorrow – nothing intensive, just hitting a few balls and getting my feet moving and the ankle working, either indoors or outdoors, and preparing mentally for the challenge ahead.

Wednesday 4 December. Adelaide.

I got back on the training paddock today, so at least that puts an end to any public queries about whether or not I will be playing in the Test match. We had our usual top-up session, with individual players receiving precisely what they needed. For me, it was about training and doing all the right things for my foot. During some light batting and slips catching practice, I felt no pain.

After training, we announced our team, and I held the captain's press conference. These conditions are going to be very different from Brisbane, so we will have to think through how we want to take our wickets in a way that is tailored to the pitch and weather we find here. Without the same bounce, we won't expect to shake England up with the short ball quite as much as in Brisbane, but Mitch Johnson has shown in England and India in one-day cricket that he can be just as effective with the shock bouncer on flat wickets as he can in more helpful conditions. I will have to be judicious in the way I use him.

There is a building rumour out now that England will play two spinners, Panesar and Swann, instead of three specialist seamers. Time will tell, but we are confident and well prepared for either eventuality.

Thursday 5 December. Adelaide.

Whatever happened in the cricket, the most important thing to acknowledge today was that we paid our respects to the North family. Marcus North is a former

Australian teammate of ours and a terrific bloke, and his elder brother Luke was tragically killed in a traffic accident in Western Australia only a few days ago. Marcus is a special member of the cricket fraternity in Australia, and a lot of us have been sending him messages of condolence this week. I contacted the North family and asked if they would give their permission for us to wear black armbands for them. They were very appreciative. Our hearts go out to Northy and all of his family and friends.

When it came to the cricket, I felt it was a crucial toss to win today. The drop-in wicket looked like it was ready for play three days ago, so I would expect it to be at its best for batting in the first innings. I was desperately hoping to win the toss, but, that said, we were also preparing for it to go either way. Whatever we did first, we had to do it well.

I was all smiles when Alastair Cook called incorrectly. Now that we have played a day, I am not sure if it is such a massive advantage to bat first on this wicket, but certainly at the time of the toss I thought it was, so I had no hesitation in putting England out in the field. They made two changes to their team from the First Test match. Tim Bresnan did not replace Chris Tremlett, as I had thought he might earlier in the week. Instead they brought in Monty Panesar, obviously feeling that the wicket would be helpful to finger-spin. To bolster their seam-bowling stocks, they brought in the young all-rounder Ben Stokes for his debut Test match to replace Jonathan Trott. They will have to rearrange their batting order, as Stokes is not a like-for-like replacement for Trott at number three. The current suggestion is that Joe Root will move up to three while Stokes will slot in at number six.

Chris Rogers and Davey Warner immediately noticed the lack of pace in the wicket, compared with Brisbane. They were on and off for short rain delays in the first session and passed on their observations about how the surface was playing. When they got back on, Davey played some nice aggressive shots off James Anderson and Stuart Broad, while also having a few challenging moments with a close LBW appeal and shots going in the air. Eventually, he couldn't get over the top of a cut shot and was out to Broad for 29, a lot less than he had set his sights on.

Shane Watson and Bucky Rogers batted extremely well together. It was a pitch that wasn't unlike some of what we played on in England, slow and kind of furry on top, with inconsistent bounce and pace. Watto played very straight and watchfully to the pacemen, and then when Graeme Swann came on in the 14th over Watto used his feet nicely.

They stayed together until the 52nd over. Chris brought up his half-century by cutting Broad to the boundary, and Watto hit some brilliant off-drives off the spinners. It was all going well until at 1/155 Anderson bowled a ball that held up a little on Watto, and he drove it back down the wicket for the bowler to hold a sharp, low chance. It was a good 50, on a day when three guys made half-centuries but each would feel that they should have got more.

The weather remained cool, and I was in long sleeves and a vest when I went out to bat before tea. Before I had even faced a ball, we were three down when Swann got one to turn sharply away from Bucky, who edged it to Matt Prior.

Things were suddenly looking shaky for us. It was hard to score and I was feeling a bit flat and like I wasn't moving my feet well. Sometimes this happens for reasons you can't quite put your finger on. Cook brought Panesar on immediately after my arrival at the crease, and I survived an appeal for caught behind when my bat scraped the ground instead of the ball. Just before tea, three down became four down when Smithy was bowled by Panesar.

The wickets were falling in the middle of our innings yet again. These are the challenges we have generally failed to meet this year. We lose one wicket, and it turns into two, three, four, five, and before we know it we have been bowled out for a substandard score. When we came back from tea, George Bailey and I were determined not to throw our wickets away. I still wasn't feeling quite right, but sometimes when you are like this it can help to focus the mind. There have been plenty of batsmen who have scored amazing Test centuries while carrying injuries, for example. And there have been many days, for me and others, when you go out to bat feeling absolutely tip-top, ready to tear the bowling apart, and before you know it you are walking back to the pavilion. So I just knuckled down and tried to take it one ball at a time. Anderson bowled tightly to me, and I did everything I could to keep him out. Meanwhile, George took the attack up to Panesar, backing himself to loft the ball down the ground when Monty gave it more air.

I could have been out on 18, when I hit a drive off Swann in the air, about knee-high, to mid-wicket. Joe Root leapt and did well to get a hand to it, but put it down. It would have been a very good catch, but even so I had to tell myself to keep my concentration. It was proving much harder to score than I had expected, and a challenge to remain patient. Then, on 23, I was only centimetres from being run out when George hit a ball down the wicket and Swann deflected it onto the stumps. You have to have your wits about you at both ends!

When England took the new ball in the 81st over, it felt as if it began to bounce a bit more truly and the scoring grew marginally easier. I got Anderson away over mid-wicket, and George absolutely flushed a pull shot off Broad, bringing up his 50 with a six. It was very special for George to make his first Test match half-century, but it was over too soon, when Broad dropped short again and George helped it on its way behind square leg, only to find Swann waiting for it.

All in all, today was one of those days when both teams will think they almost got on top but didn't quite manage it. We would have liked a few more runs than our 273 and a few less wickets down than the five we lost, but the pitch and outfield were slow, and after that pre-tea mini-collapse there was every chance we could be bowled out, so we have to be grateful that we're five wickets down and very much in the match. For England, they would be quite happy, but Michael Carberry dropped Brad Haddin in the second-last over off the bowling of Panesar, a straightforward chance behind point, and that would be eating away at them. They also put me down with that one half-chance to Joe Root, so it will be up to Hadds and me to make the most of our good fortune.

My thoughts tonight are that we need 350-plus, which is another 78 runs, to be relatively satisfied. I will be happy if we can get past that.

Friday 6 December. Adelaide.

When I woke up this morning, I felt a lot more energetic than yesterday. I went to the ground early and had some hot and cold baths to freshen my legs up, and then went into the nets out the back of the changing rooms to have a hit. I didn't feel that I batted very well yesterday, and was keen to get into the middle and show my intent.

Brad Haddin was in the same mood. What's new? When he bats, Hadds is nearly always bristling with positive energy. The weather was warmer this morning, and it was one of those days that just had a good feeling about it. To the first ball of the day, bowled by Stuart Broad from the Cathedral end, Hadds played a beautiful cover drive. We were in the frame of mind to push our score along.

I nearly brought it all undone with the first ball I faced today. Monty Panesar was bowling from the River end, and I went down the wicket to drive him. I caught it on the thick outside edge, and it ballooned up towards cover. I could tell when I hit it that it was going to clear the field, but only just. Having survived that, I had a good sense about the way we were going. I kept coming down the pitch to Panesar, and got a better drive away over mid-on, and then played a few cuts and drives along the ground through the infield. One thing about Adelaide hasn't changed, which is that if you time the ball well square of the wicket and get it through the cordon of fieldsmen, you will almost always be rewarded with a boundary.

Hadds was steady, while maintaining his positive intent. Our only other concern in that first period was when I cut Panesar behind point and shouted 'Yes!' for a run before really assessing the situation.

Hadds responded, charging down the wicket for a run that suddenly didn't look like it was there. When your partner calls you for a bad run, as I did to Hadds, hesitation is death; you just have to trust him and run. He was too far down for me to send him back, so I took off as well. Luckily for us, Carberry's throw wasn't accurate and Hadds made it home. The last thing we wanted, when we were feeling so good, was a run-out.

By drinks, we were nearly up to the 350 mark. Swann bowled an eventful over after the break. Hadds swept him and got a top edge, but still made good enough contact for the ball to sail over square leg for six. He took a single to put me on strike, and next ball I went down the wicket. Swann turned it in from the off, and, not quite to the pitch of it, I clipped it to the leg-side where Ian Bell was fielding close in. As with Root yesterday, it would have been a sensational catch, but Bell put it down, and then just missed the stumps when he tried to flick it in and run me out. I don't believe too much in 'lucky days', but if England were beginning to feel that the rub of the green was going against them, all the better for us.

It wasn't long afterwards that they really must have been questioning what they had done to anger the cricket gods. Their debutant all-rounder, the red-haired Ben Stokes, had been bowling some willing fast-medium stuff, and he sent down the ball of the day to Hadds. It nipped away, caught the edge, and went through to

Matt Prior. Hadds was walking off when the umpire asked to check on a front-foot no-ball, which has become fairly routine in the game. When they had another look, the officials found that Stokes had over-stepped. It's a tough call on a kid still waiting for his first Test wicket, and even tougher for him to think that he has it, only to have it taken away. But we have had our share of wickets reversed through front-foot no-balls, and have worked our backsides off to address this issue of discipline. So I don't have too much sympathy!

After lunch, Hadds and I resumed with more caution than in the morning. Anderson bowled a good spell first-up, working at getting some reverse swing. I was moving my feet better now, and after I hit him for a straight four he was replaced by Broad. Hadds was beginning to blossom against the spinners, increasing his rate of scoring, and we were able to negate any plan England might have had to tie us down and stop us from rotating the strike. I didn't have any more major scares apart from another straight drive from Hadds that Panesar nearly touched onto the stumps while I was backing up. Hadds is such a sweet straight driver of the ball, I should have been more careful.

The partnership, which came to 200 all up, was a record for the sixth wicket at Adelaide. It's a thrill to be in the record books alongside Brad Haddin, and always a nice experience batting with him. We started playing cricket together when I was 17, we've been through a lot of highs and lows, we trained a lot together for New South Wales before we broke into Test cricket, and we know how hard each other has worked growing up. It's just a delight to get the opportunity to bat with him in Test cricket and do well for our team when they need us.

And we could have made more! A moment of laziness got me out. Stokes bowled a bit of a nothing ball on my hip, which I closed the face on and popped up a catch. A score of 148 was good enough to make me happy, for sure, but I left the ground feeling a bit unsatisfied. There was the chance to make a really big one, and I left it out there.

Mitch Johnson came and went quickly, but Hadds proceeded to his fourth Test century, his third against England. I couldn't be happier for him. He went excruciatingly close to getting us home at Trent Bridge in July, and batted well right through the series in England. At home, he's had a fantastic start, leading by example as vice-captain. He deserved a hundred in Brisbane, and now he has one here. What a player.

Nobody takes himself more seriously as a batsman than Ryan Harris, who went out there and set about putting on a bonus partnership with Hadds. In the nets we call Ryan 'Jacques Kallis', because he's so dedicated and spends so long with a bat in his hands. He still knows to bat for the team, though, and today he didn't stuff around. He scored a half-century, his second in Tests, at a rate of a run a ball. His late hitting enabled me to declare at 9/570, leaving us about an hour to bowl at England before stumps. Considering I'd been hoping for 350 this morning, it was a great result.

So we had about 15 overs in which to throw ourselves at England and, we hoped, get a wicket or two. I think I said earlier that Stokes's ball to Hadds, the no-ball, was the best delivery of the day. I mean while we were batting. Mitch Johnson bowled what was without doubt the ball of the day, maybe of the series so far, in his second over to Alastair Cook. From ball one, Mitch's pace was up close to the 150 kilometres an hour zone, and Cook had been keen to get off strike. Mitch bowled a pearler, with some really nice shape at high pace, and it knocked over Cook's off stump. It was the start we wanted, to say the least.

Our bowlers put in an excellent effort in the next hour, which Michael Carberry and Joe Root were possibly lucky to survive. Mitch hit Root in the chest with a ball that hurt enough to make you wince, even if you were watching from second slip. Then, in the last over, Root was keen to get off strike to Mitch and called Carberry through for a single he was never going to make. Unfortunately for us, Bucky Rogers's throw missed.

Then, on the last ball, Carberry moved across his stumps and was hit on the pad. Mitch appealed, and the umpire gave it not out. We had a brief chat, but Hadds had been moving towards the leg-side. Mitch wasn't sure, while Hadds said he thought it was missing leg. It wasn't until after we went off the ground that we saw the replays indicating that if we had referred the decision, Carberry would have been given out.

So a very good day would have been a great day if I had found a way to refer that last one. All the same, we are now in a position to drive the advantage home. We still have 19 wickets to take to win the Test match, in what are sure to be favourable conditions for the batsmen, but if there's one thing I know about our bowling attack it's that they are prepared to work.

Saturday 7 December. Adelaide.

What an amazing day. I can't remember too many bowling spells that have matched the pace and accuracy of Mitchell Johnson's today. It was unbelievable, and I certainly didn't expect it. The wicket was still good for batting, and I thought it would be a tough grind for us to bowl all day to try to get nine more wickets. At best, I was hoping we would have England out by stumps. We have ended up with much better than that.

In warmer weather, the day started calmly enough. Ryan Harris and Mitch started with three maidens, and only five runs came from their first six overs. Joe Root and Michael Carberry were playing cautiously, to see off the big threats of our new-ball bowlers, but we were also happy to be tying them down and building up some scoreboard pressure.

The mood of the innings began to change when I brought Nathan Lyon on from the River end. He had Carberry in a bit of strife in his first over, with a near-catch close in and another that went past the edge. Carberry got him away once, but it was with a fairly wild shot to the on-side. In Nathan's next over, Root didn't wait to have a go at him. To Nathan's first ball, Root got on his knee and slog-swept. It flew quite high, but Chris Rogers judged it very well running in from deep square leg and took the catch.

Kevin Pietersen came in, and it happened to be time to bring Peter Siddle on. Sidds proceeded to bowl an extremely good tight spell from the Cathedral end. We went up for a big caught-behind appeal before Pietersen had scored, and Hadds was confident so I referred the not-out decision. Unhappily for us, the replay showed Pietersen's bat scraping his pad, so he wasn't out. But Sidds kept steaming in and Pietersen scored runs off his outside edge, then off his inside edge, and then Sidds swung one in that went straight through him, agonisingly close to the off bail. Sidds was creating chances. If he kept bowling like this, the wicket had to come.

We had what has become a standard field setting for Pietersen in certain conditions, with two men at close catching short mid-wicket positions. They are not orthodox positions for most batsmen, but we have had some success with those fielders in place for Pietersen, especially when he's facing Sidds. Sure enough, Sidds had bowled so well at him to build up so much pressure, Pietersen decided to be positive and stepped across his stumps towards the off-side. He clipped the ball to leg, where it went quite fast above George Bailey's head. George stuck up a hand and parried it into the air. We held our breath as he juggled it three or four times and then, with a big smile on his face, brought it in. Sidds was ecstatic, as was everyone in our team and a solid majority of the big Adelaide Oval crowd.

Two key wickets before lunch were just what we needed, but Carberry was looking quite settled and the new man was Bell, whose abilities we know all too well. The next hour could, we thought, prove crucial to the course of the match. Bell played positively against Nathan Lyon, lifting him for a straight six and racing into the twenties. Carberry was getting on the front foot and driving well, apparently comfortable against Sidds, and before we knew it the two of them had put on 40-odd runs and Carberry had his maiden Test half-century.

I made a double change, bringing on Ryan Harris from the Cathedral end and Shane Watson from the River end. The effect was immediate. Rhino had Bell under-edging, and playing and missing. The scoring dried up completely as Watto tied Carberry down. For over after over, each bowler's accuracy was allowing the other to work on his man: Rhino had Bell, and Watto had Carberry.

We changed our plan of attack to Bell, aiming more at the stumps, so I moved a couple of catchers from the slips cordon to the pair of short mid-wickets we had had for Pietersen. Rhino bowled a couple of super-sharp bouncers at Bell, one bending him backwards and the other hitting him on the gloves. It was fantastic bowling, and Rhino and Watto deserve a lot of credit for the wickets Mitch was later able to get.

After 30 dot balls in a row from both bowlers combined, Watto dropped short to Carberry. He jumped all over it, and to be honest he hit his pull shot well. Few fielders could have caught it, but Davey Warner, the squarer of the two short mid-wickets, dived to his left and caught the ball one-handed as it was going past him. Any batsman could sympathise with Carberry's disappointment, but we converged on Davey and Watto and were understandably euphoric.

This, we felt, could be the crack. I brought Mitch on for one over before lunch, and Bell got a streaky cut away over slips. The other batsman was Ben Stokes, playing his first Test innings, so we knew he would be nervous. We were feeling confident at lunch, and after the break Mitch, who had bowled lightly in the morning session, was well rested and ready to tear in from the Cathedral end.

Stokes got his first run with a stolen single that might have been a run-out but for a misfield. You could sense the tension now that Mitch was on. The new stands in Adelaide amplify the sound of the crowd much more than in the past, and, just as we did in Brisbane, we felt the swell of support from the stands. ASICS' marketing slogan for the summer is 'This time they'll have to beat a whole nation', or words to that effect, and it feels that way at times like this. It's the England cricket team against the whole of Australia. With the first ball of his next over, Mitch hit Stokes on the pad. The umpire gave it not out, but we all thought it looked very close and certainly worth referring. And so it proved.

Mitch was getting on a roll now. You could feel that wickets were coming. To Matt Prior he bowled a brilliant sequence: bouncer, bouncer, then a jaffa that had him playing forward and nicking. It was as good a three-ball streak as he bowled to Carberry in the first innings in Brisbane. Sensational. Stuart Broad came in, and stopped the game for six minutes while something, a reflection I think, was rectified on the Cathedral end sightscreen. Mitch hurled one in and scattered Broad's stumps – a six-minute golden duck. In that one over, Mitch had taken three wickets with some fast bowling that you were pretty glad you didn't have to face.

His next over was kept out by Bell, but we managed to get Graeme Swann on strike for the beginning of Mitch's next over. Sure enough, Swann was out edging to me at second slip and then James Anderson was out first ball. For the second time in about 15 minutes, Mitch was on a hat-trick.

He didn't get it, and in fact the next hour went pretty quiet for us. Monty Panesar got in behind the ball, and

Bell was in good touch. I dropped a straightforward chance, Panesar nicking Nathan Lyon to first slip. The fact that Bell and Panesar hung around for an hour affected the match as a whole. Mitch had had such irresistible momentum that when he took the ninth wicket I was seriously considering enforcing the follow-on, getting England back out there batting again while they were still undoubtedly shell-shocked. We had only bowled 55 overs by then, and our attack was fresh. But during the hour that Panesar and Bell stuck around, I began to feel that our bowlers might need a break, and there was every indication that the wicket was still good for batting. We were a long way ahead, almost 400 runs, but I felt that if our bowlers were tired we might be biting off more than we could chew by sending England in again. Also, it's only the Second Test and we have another, back-to-back, starting later this week in Perth. I have to consider these things. By the time Mitch bowled Panesar, I had decided to bat instead of making England follow on.

It has to be said that Mitch's spell today was as good as I have ever seen in cricket. The pitch had no pace, yet he was terrifyingly fast and accurate. He couldn't have done it without the other bowlers knowing their role and tying the batsmen down, or, as Nathan Lyon did in his last over, keeping Bell on strike so that Mitch could have a crack at Panesar. Two balls later, the innings was over. These guys really are bowling for each other. The other bowlers are happy that Mitch is taking the wickets, because the wickets belong to all of us. It's certainly nobody's role *not* to get wickets. The aim is to get 20 per Test, and we don't care who takes them.

So we were batting again, and all of a sudden the so-called placid batsmen's paradise was not easy at all. Anderson got Chris Rogers caught behind in his second over, and two balls later Shane Watson was caught at backward point. We were two wickets for four runs when I joined Davey. It doesn't matter what the situation is, Test cricket is never as simple as it might look. Davey and I knuckled down and batted positively for about an hour, before Panesar beat me with a good ball turning past the outside edge and hitting the stumps.

It's always tempting to have a little crack at opening batsmen before stumps, but I felt that our bowlers had done enough today, and decided to bat through to the end of the day. The Perth Test match starts on Friday. There are five Test matches for us to win, and winning the Ashes is what counts. I can't get over-aggressive and throw everything at this final session when our bowlers need to put their feet up. We still have two full days left, and the weather forecast is pretty good . . . fingers crossed. I expect we will do a bit more batting tomorrow. Davey is 83 not out overnight and looks a good thing to make a hundred. I would love to see him make it, and there's no question that he deserves it. A few more runs, an extended break for the bowlers, and then we can get England in again.

Sunday 8 December. Adelaide.

When I woke up this morning, everything had changed. I watched the *Today* show, to tune in to the weather forecast, and they were talking about rain in Adelaide today and tomorrow. Rain and cool weather! It really is turning into an unusual Test match for this city.

As soon as I got to the Adelaide Oval, I talked to the ground staff and had a look at their radar. They agreed that there was plenty of rain about, particularly in the back half of today and throughout tomorrow.

This turned my plans upside down. Initially I had wanted to bat for another ten to 15 overs today, for different reasons. There was the opportunity for David Warner to convert his unbeaten 83 into a century, which he deserved so much. I also liked the idea of keeping England out in the field for an extra hour, and of letting our bowlers have a bit more rest so they would not have to start their work with a full two-hour pre-lunch session and a likely full day's bowling to follow.

Anyway, that was the theory, but the forecasts forced me to change my mind. Nothing would be more frustrating than to dominate this match in the way we have and not leave with the 2–0 lead we think we deserve. For England to get out of here with a draw would be as morale-boosting as a win for them.

All of this added up to me telling Davey I was going to declare immediately, on our overnight score, before the start of play. He wasn't bothered one bit. He just said, 'Do whatever's best for the team.' That was pleasing to hear. He really did deserve that hundred for the way he batted yesterday afternoon, but it's a sweet sound to a captain's ears when a player is so quick to lay aside his personal ambition for the team's sake.

About 25 minutes before the scheduled start of play, I began walking towards the visitors' dressing room. On my way through the lunch room, I ran into England's team director, Andy Flower, and told him we were declaring. He said he would take the message to Alastair Cook. Flower didn't seem at all surprised.

The wicket is still pretty flat, so we knew we had a lot of grinding toil ahead of us. Our lead was 530, probably out of England's reach, but in the conditions they would have started their innings feeling they could bat out a draw. Ryan Harris started with some really good full-pitched bowling from the River end, and then we had an unbelievable breakthrough. Mitch's third ball in his first over from the Cathedral end to Cook was a head-high bouncer, and Cook went for the hook shot. He plays the shot well, but this time he couldn't get over the top of it and it flew off the top edge. Rhino was down there at fine leg, one of the safest outfield catchers, and we were jubilant when he duly took the chance. Nine wickets to go, and one of the toughest was already out of the way on the ninth ball of the innings.

As amazing as it was to get this breakthrough, we had to stick to our plans. I took Mitch off after a three-over spell. Michael Carberry and Joe Root were doing well to keep him out. Sidds came on, and Rhino bowled an outstanding first spell with some really sharp well-directed bouncers before I gave him a rest and brought on Nathan Lyon from the River end. He got some turn, albeit slow, straight away. We had a flash of hope when Carberry drove Nathan's fourth ball straight into the groin of George Bailey, who was at silly point. It popped out again; it wasn't a genuine chance, but sometimes those ones stick.

For Sidds, I had Nathan positioned fairly square at fine leg, almost at deep backward square. Carberry is a confident puller and hooker, and goes for the shot when he sees it. But we always think we're in with a chance of getting him with a leg-side catch. In Sidds's third over, he bowled a short ball which Carberry hooked cleanly but in the air. As with all of the boys, Nathan has become a much improved outfielder under the coaching of Mike Young and Steve Rixon, and he made the catch look easier than it was. Not yet an hour in, and we had England two down.

The clouds were gathering overhead, however, and I was acutely conscious of the possibility that we might not get a full day's play in. With Kevin Pietersen joining Root, we had another battle on our hands. Both batsmen were in a determined mood. Nathan and Sidds kept

My back injury had flared up just before the First Test. But after a lot of medical and physio treatment, I was back in the nets – putting a smile on my face.

The day before the First Test match, everyone went through their own routines with laying out their gear in the Gabba changing room. I suppose I'm neater than some – as you can see, there's a lot of stuff, and if I didn't keep some sense of order I'd go crazy.

From day one in Brisbane, Stuart Broad stood up as the most dangerous English bowler. Here he celebrates after dismissing Mitch Johnson.

In the 'red zone' before lunch, we got Jonathan Trott out caught down the leg side. His face shows some of the disappointment – and stress that we weren't yet aware he was suffering.

There were lots of small changes to the 'new' Mitchell Johnson we saw in Brisbane. They all added up to one big change, which was a complete focus and self-confidence. I was glad I only had to face him in the nets.

After my first-innings failure, I was elated to score a century in Brisbane. All a matter of trusting my plans.

My wife Kyly enjoyed my century as much as I did.

I had the best seat in the house to watch David Warner's wonderful Brisbane hundred. He always knows how to enjoy the moment.

I wasn't very proud of the language I used with James Anderson on the fourth afternoon in Brisbane, but was only sticking up for my teammate George Bailey. It showed that even though this Test match was almost over, we were going to be relentless until the end of the series. We hadn't won anything yet.

One down! We believed we could beat England, but only when we took the last wicket in Brisbane did we know it for sure.

Having been in the same shoes a few months earlier, I knew a little of what Alastair Cook was going through.

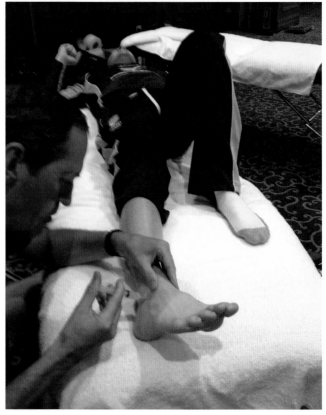

Doctor Peter Brukner gives me a painkilling injection into the ankle I rolled before the Adelaide Test match. I was far from the only Australian player who saw a lot of the Doc, and he was largely responsible for getting us through the series with the same eleven players.

Me and my faithful friend, the MedX machine.

We took the field in Adelaide wearing black armbands as a sign of respect for our mate Marcus North's tragic loss of his brother.

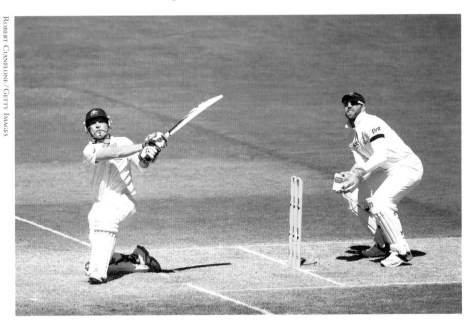

Brad Haddin and I have played together since we were teenagers. It was a career highlight to be with him as we put on some big runs in Adelaide.

Not without some anxious moments, I made it to a second hundred for the series in Adelaide. With runs on the board, we now had England on the defensive.

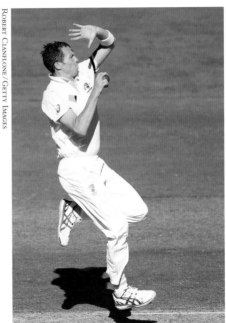

Our pace bowling cartel. In the first innings on a dead track in Adelaide, Mitch Johnson (*top left*) bowled one of the best spells I have ever seen. In the second innings, Peter Siddle (*top right*) and Ryan Harris (*bottom*) had their turn to be among the wickets.

Ready for action. In Perth as we are taking the field, you can see the determination on our faces. Knowing how much was on the line, we were sticking to our mantra in the field of treating every single run as if the Ashes depended on it. Looking back, a 5–0 win appears one-sided. But at the time, I was as nervous as I have ever been during a cricket match.

Alastair and I both reached 100 Tests in Perth. Unlike Brisbane and Adelaide, this was a toss that I wasn't too concerned about losing. As it happened, I won my third in a row.

At the end of the Perth Test match, the team gave me this photo, framed, to commemorate my 100th Test appearance for my country. I will treasure it forever.

Will Russell / Getty Images

Late on the second afternoon in Perth, England were digging in and I thought it was time to motivate the crowd. They responded beautifully, which powered our bowlers to take some vital wickets.

Robert Cianflone / Getty Images

Shane Watson made a steady start to his second innings in Perth on the third afternoon. The next morning, he exploded with some unforgettable hitting.

It was a toss of a coin, in the end, between Mitch Johnson and Brad Haddin for man of the series. Hadds was not only making history with the bat, but his catching and all-round keeping was close to flawless. This speccy dismissed Joe Root.

We've returned the urn! George Bailey, who was always reliable close-in, takes the final catch to dismiss James Anderson off Mitch Johnson's bowling. In the background, you can see Nathan Lyon already warming up his vocal chords.

What a feeling! Everyone in that group knows he played a vital role in creating one of the biggest turnarounds in Ashes history.

Darren Lehmann deserves all the credit he was given. He became our coach in May during trying circumstances in England, and put his aims into one word: 'Winning.' Seven months later, we'd won!

Shane Warne knows how to put on a party, and he hosted the team and our partners at Crown Metropol in Burswood after we won the Test match. Thanks mate!

testing their patience through the middle of the session, but they resisted and I brought Mitch back on for a short spell before lunch from the Cathedral end, while Shane Watson had his first bowl of the day from the River end. They both had a few hopeful moments, going past Root's edge a couple of times, and Mitch varied his angle to the right-hander by coming around the wicket. Hadds also decided to stand up to the stumps to Watto, having spotted how keen the English batsmen were to get forward. But no further wickets fell before lunch, not even when I brought back Nathan and the joker in the pack, Steve Smith with his leg-spin, for a couple of overs before the end of the session.

After the break we pursued our plan of accumulating dot balls and trying the batsmen's patience. Rhino and Mitch bowled accurate spells, doing just that. To see if something might come of it, I gave Smithy another bowl, from the River end. It got a bit interesting for a while. Pietersen hit Smithy's first ball, a rank full toss, over wide mid-on for six. In Smithy's next over, Pietersen again came down the track and skied a drive off the leading edge, landing it just over mid-off who was running back. Then Smithy, as is his habit, landed a leg break that Shane Warne would have been proud of, going past Pietersen's outside edge and just missing the off stump. Smithy followed it with a full toss, which Pietersen hit down the ground and ran, testing Davey Warner's arm. Davey hit the stumps at the bowler's end, but Pietersen was just safe. Soon after, Pietersen hit two sixes off Smithy to raise his half-century, and England had got through the hour without losing a wicket. I kept looking at the sky, wondering when that forecast rain was going to come, and gradually grew more tense as Root and Pietersen built their partnership.

Sidds and Watto resumed the attack after the drinks break. It was back to basics for us, building pressure, grinding the batsmen down. Pietersen looked a bit sketchy against Sidds, chipping balls in the air either side of the short mid-wicket I had placed. Then, in the 48th over of the innings, Sidds did what he does so well, reserving his best for Pietersen. He nipped one in that Pietersen inside-edged just in time. Next ball, Pietersen came well forward, and Sidds bowled him one tight against his hip. The ball looked like it was rising over the off stump. Pietersen likes to play forward a lot, and uses his height to get over the top of balls that most batsmen would need to play off the back foot. This time, the ball was too high to control, and he only managed to steer it down with the inside edge. The ball just grazed the top of the bails. You could see Pietersen right up on his toes, willing the ball to pass over. But he was out, for 53, and once again Sidds had his man.

This opened the door, but we have chased too many balls hit by Ian Bell this year to take anything for granted. Root was really digging in, playing cautiously and not giving us many chances. We nearly had him run out, when Bell took a chancy single to get off the mark, but Rhino's throw just missed the stumps. The English pair stuck together for half an hour, with their eye on the tea break, and I just had a hunch about Smithy, who had created a few chances earlier and, as we all remember, dismissed Bell twice in England. Smithy, in fact, has made sure no one forgets it! He tells anyone who will listen that Ian Bell is his 'bunny'. He says he's got Bell out nine times in his career. Somebody in the changing room has gone away to fact-check that one. It turns out that Smithy had actually only got Bell out four times: one was in junior cricket, one was when Bell had scored 195 in the innings, one was caught on the boundary, and one was a run-out off Smithy's bowling that he was laying claim to. Still, you can't fault his confidence!

His fourth ball was a pretty ropy full toss, but the thing with wrist spinners is, they put so many revs on the ball that it can drop fast in the air. Bell came down the wicket to smash it to the boundary, but got his timing a bit wrong and scooped his drive to mid-on. Mitch Johnson, who rarely puts down a chance, got his hands under the ball, which flew fairly flat and fast. Our celebrations were as raucous as they usually are when a big wicket falls to one of the lesser-rated bowlers. And then Smithy nearly had another scalp, when Ben Stokes glanced his second ball to George Bailey at short leg; again, it was one of those not-even-half chances that either sticks or doesn't. If it had, we would never have heard the end of it from Smithy, who was probably ready to claim that he had got Stokes out ten times before.

Having collected those two prize wickets, Pietersen and Bell, in the session we were quite upbeat at tea. But Root and Stokes are tough young cricketers and we knew that our work was far from finished. I noticed that the skies had lifted a little, though rain was hovering in the area around central Adelaide and about half an hour after tea the floodlights came on.

I started the session with Mitch and Nathan, soon replacing Mitch with Rhino. The seamers kept it tight, and there was some more action when Nathan was bowling. Root put away a couple of short balls, but then Nathan was desperately unlucky not to get him when an inside edge slipped past the leg stump.

A couple of overs later, Lyono had his man. Root went forward and then back, pushing down defensively, inside-edging onto his thigh. The ball popped up for an instant, and Hadds swooped, diving in front of the stumps and cupping his right glove under the ball. It was a catch Hadds would always back himself to take, but also a continuation of what is becoming one of the best summers of his life. We were absolutely overjoyed to have got rid of Root, who had occupied the crease for the best part of five hours.

Rhino, meanwhile, was bowling an excellent spell to test out Stokes in his second Test innings. He hit him fairly close to adjacent, and made a big LBW appeal.

The umpire gave it not out, and Rhino was insistent. We were not overwhelmingly confident, but it was close enough to give a referral a shot, as we knew we would have our referrals replenished in about an hour, when the 80th over came up. Unfortunately, this one wasn't out, and a couple of overs later Rhino hit Stokes in front again but had no referrals left. That second one would have been closer. In his frustration, Rhino threw the ball at the stumps, missed, and it went for four overthrows, to rub salt into the wound.

To save the pacemen for the second new ball, I gave Smithy and Lyono a little spell of spin from both ends. Stokes and Matt Prior batted watchfully, though Stokes turned yet another one in the direction of George Bailey at bat–pad, and again it didn't stick. Another wicket, we knew, and we were just about there.

The sun came out at the time we took the second new ball, a good sign that the weather was not going to turn foul on us. Mitch and Rhino steamed in, and there was a minor incident when Mitch and Stokes brushed each other's shoulders as the Englishman took a run. There wasn't anything in it, both players being within their rights to hold their line, so while I am sure a bit will be said about it, I'm confident that the match referee will apply common sense. These things happen in cricket. They can look ugly when captured in a photo that ends up on the back page, but most of the time they happen quickly and don't raise any real heat or controversy on the field.

The crucial wicket, the one that would expose the tail, was tantalisingly close. Prior lost sight of a yorker Mitch bowled from the Cathedral end, leaving it unplayed while it went within a whisper of his off stump. So close!

Rhino had definitely been the unlucky bowler through the afternoon, and he was bowling with typical persistence through the pain of a flare-up in his chronically sore right knee. In his third over with the second new ball, he got his reward in his usual fashion, putting the ball right on the spot for Stokes to push at uncertainly. The edge flew comfortably to me at second slip and we were into the bowlers.

Nevertheless, Prior and Stuart Broad survived till stumps, batting quite well. I would have loved for the game to be over today, not because I don't think we can take the remaining four wickets but because I am still worried about the rain tomorrow. Still, we are in a fantastic position and if the day is not washed out I am hopeful that we will win and go 2–0 up.

Monday 9 December. Adelaide.

Not a good start to the day! When I woke up this morning, the first thing I did was open my curtains to see what the weather was like. The second thing I did was to pull them shut again. It was raining lightly but persistently, and the sky had that heavy, still look that suggested the rain was set in. It's just about the worst sight you could have seen. I have been thinking more and more about how comprehensively we have outplayed England in this match, and how extremely disappointing it would be if we don't get a win out of it. The English would be delighted to escape with a draw, and would go to Perth with their spirits up. When you are playing two Test matches so close together, starting just three days apart, the momentum you take from one into the next can be crucial. We saw that last year, when we dominated the match in Adelaide but couldn't put South Africa away on the last day. They went to Perth with their tails up, as if the draw had been a win, and we were flat and down on energy. They outplayed us in Perth, but their momentum had started when they escaped with the draw in Adelaide.

Anyway, it hasn't happened that way this summer. I am relieved, and extremely pleased, that we have converted our dominance into a win here.

As the morning wore on, the rain gradually lightened. It was still wet when we got to the ground, but the Adelaide Oval staff did a terrific job, drying out the grass as soon as the rain let up. Contrary to all my fears, we got on at the scheduled start time of 10.30 am. So full credit to the ground staff, even though the playing surface was still a bit damp.

Things happened quickly on the field. Stuart Broad was facing Peter Siddle, bowling from the River end, with a ball that was only ten overs old. The fourth ball of the morning was a bouncer that Broad hit sweetly over mid-wicket for six. Next ball was a bit faster and higher, and Broad tried to repeat the stroke. The sure hands of Nathan Lyon were waiting under it near the fence, and our first wicket had only taken five balls.

It was that kind of morning, when the cricket was played at an accelerated pace. Matt Prior punched a couple of boundaries through the off-side, struck some well-timed pull shots, but also played and missed at Mitch Johnson fairly regularly. Graeme Swann was trying his best to get behind the shorter balls, and soon I replaced Mitch with Ryan Harris. It only took him three balls to get a good one rising on the line of off stump, which Swann edged to me at second slip. Next over, Prior became another of the many English batsmen to be caught in the outfield on the leg-side, hooking Sidds away to Rhino at deep backward square, and Monty Panesar wasn't going to hold us up for another hour, giving Rhino his third wicket of the innings, caught by Chris Rogers.

My most powerful feeling, as we celebrated, was relief. It's a fantastic Test win, but I had become so worked up with anxiety over the weather that I just felt a great release of tension.

Mitch won the man of the match award again, and he deserves it richly. His spell in the first innings will not be forgotten for a long time. That wicket was flat and slow, and for him to rip through the English middle order and create such panic in a few overs was the performance that swung the match.

That said, I felt that Peter Siddle, Ryan Harris, Shane Watson, Nathan Lyon and Steve Smith were all outstanding with the ball in their different ways. I look around the dressing room and I see eleven guys who have made important individual contributions, with bat, with ball, and in the field. Every guy sitting here can feel that he played a role in this win, as was the case in Brisbane too. If I could put my happiness in a nutshell, that's it – the confidence that we are playing a fine, aggressive brand of cricket from number one down to number eleven.

There is probably a fair bit of surprise out in the public that after losing 3–0 in England we are suddenly 2–0 ahead here. It's a wonderful feeling, but we know it's no fluke and it's no sudden turnaround. The guys have worked so hard for a long time, they know they are doing nothing more or less than reaping the rewards for something that has been a long time in the making. Some of them have had to overcome great adversity, whether it's Hadds being out of the team last year for personal reasons, Mitch being out of the team for a lengthy time before he fought so hard to get back in, or Davey, who was dropped for off-field reasons in England but wanted so much to be a part of this team.

Everyone has a story that is as special as everyone else's. I could not be happier, or prouder. A lot of people looked at the Adelaide Oval and the drop-in wicket and predicted a draw. We certainly didn't come here for that.

Second Test
5–9 December 2013. Adelaide Oval.

Australia (first innings)

Batting		R	B	4	6	SR
CJL Rogers	c: Prior b: Swann	72	167	11	0	43.11
DA Warner	c: Carberry b: Broad	29	32	4	0	90.62
SR Watson	c & b: Anderson	51	119	6	1	42.85
MJ Clarke	c: Anderson b: Stokes	148	245	17	0	60.40
SPD Smith	b: Panesar	6	17	1	0	35.29
GJ Bailey	c: Swann b: Broad	53	93	4	3	56.98
BJ Haddin	c: Prior b: Broad	118	177	11	5	66.66
MG Johnson	c: Broad b: Swann	5	13	1	0	38.46
PM Siddle	c: Prior b: Stokes	2	9	0	0	22.22
RJ Harris	not out	55	54	6	2	101.85
NM Lyon	not out	17	26	1	1	65.38
Extras	(1lb, 1w, 4nb, 8b)	14				
Total	9 Wkts, 158 overs	570		3.60 Runs/Over		

Fall of wickets 1-34 (Warner, 7.6 ov), 2-155 (Watson, 51.6 ov), 3-155 (Rogers, 52.5 ov), 4-174 (Smith, 58.3 ov), 5-257 (Bailey, 85.3 ov), 6-457 (Clarke, 136.1 ov), 7-474 (Johnson, 139.3 ov), 8-483 (Siddle, 142.3 ov), 9-529 (Haddin, 150.5 ov)

Bowling	O	M	R	W	Econ	SR	Extras
JM Anderson	30	10	85	1	2.83	180	(1nb)
SCJ Broad	30	3	98	3	3.26	60	(1w)
GP Swann	36	4	151	2	4.19	108	
MS Panesar	44	7	157	1	3.56	264	
BA Stokes	18	2	70	2	3.88	54	(3nb)

England (first innings)

Batting		R	B	4	6	SR
AN Cook	b: Johnson	3	11	0	0	27.27
MA Carberry	c: Warner b: Watson	60	144	10	0	41.66
JE Root	c: Rogers b: Lyon	15	80	1	0	18.75
KP Pietersen	c: Bailey b: Siddle	4	12	0	0	33.33
IR Bell	not out	72	106	9	4	67.92
BA Stokes	lbw: Johnson	1	12	0	0	8.33
MJ Prior	c: Haddin b: Johnson	0	4	0	0	0.00
SCJ Broad	b: Johnson	0	1	0	0	0.00
GP Swann	c: Clarke b: Johnson	7	7	0	0	100.00
JM Anderson	b: Johnson	0	1	0	0	0.00
MS Panesar	b: Johnson	2	35	0	0	5.71
Extras	[3lb, 2w, 3nb, 0b]	8				
Total	10 Wkts, 68.2 overs	172		2.51 Runs/Over		

Fall of wickets 1-9 (Cook, 2.4 ov), 2-57 (Root, 29.6 ov), 3-66 (Pietersen, 34.3 ov), 4-111 (Carberry, 45.6 ov), 5-117 (Stokes, 50.1 ov), 6-117 (Prior, 50.5 ov), 7-117 (Broad, 50.6 ov), 8-135 (Swann, 54.5 ov), 9-135 (Anderson, 54.6 ov),10-172 (Panesar, 68.2 ov)

Bowling	O	M	R	W	Econ	SR	Extras
MG Johnson	17.2	8	40	7	2.30	52	(2nb, 1w)
RJ Harris	14	8	31	0	2.21	–	
NM Lyon	20	5	64	1	3.20	120	
PM Siddle	14	4	34	1	2.42	84	(1nb, 1w)
SR Watson	3	3	0	1	0.00	18	

Australia (second innings)

Batting		R	B	4	6	SR
CJL Rogers	c: Prior b: Anderson	2	10	0	0	20.00
DA Warner	not out	83	117	9	1	70.94
SR Watson	c: Carberry b: Anderson	0	2	0	0	0.00
MJ Clarke	b: Panesar	22	51	2	0	43.13
SPD Smith	not out	23	54	2	0	42.59
GJ Bailey						
BJ Haddin						
MG Johnson						
PM Siddle						
RJ Harris						
NM Lyon						

Extras	(1lb, 0w, 0nb, 1b)	2		
Total	3 Wkts, 39 overs	132		3.38 Runs/Over

Fall of wickets 1-67 (Rogers, 23.1 ov), 2-75 (Watson, 29.3 ov), 3-233 (Warner, 58.4 ov), 4-242 (Smith, 61.4 ov),5-294 (Clarke, 74.5 ov), 6-305 (Bailey, 78.4 ov), 7-395 (Haddin, 93.1 ov)

Bowling	O	M	R	W	Econ	SR	Extras
JM Anderson	7	1	19	2	2.71	21	
SCJ Broad	6	0	19	0	3.16	–	
GP Swann	9	3	31	0	3.44	–	
BA Stokes	7	3	20	0	2.85	–	
MS Panesar	10	0	41	1	4.10	60	

England (second innings)

Batting		R	B	4	6	SR
AN Cook	c: Harris b: Johnson	1	7	0	0	14.28
MA Carberry	c: Lyon b: Siddle	14	39	2	0	35.89
JE Root	c: Haddin b: Lyon	87	194	9	0	44.84
KP Pietersen	b: Siddle	53	99	2	3	53.53
IR Bell	c: Johnson b: Smith	6	19	1	0	31.57
BA Stokes	c: Clarke b: Harris	28	90	5	0	31.11
MJ Prior	c: Harris b: Siddle	69	102	12	0	67.64
SCJ Broad	c: Lyon b: Siddle	29	26	3	1	111.53
GP Swann	c: Clarke b: Harris	6	14	0	0	42.85
JM Anderson	not out	13	14	2	0	92.85
MS Panesar	c: Rogers b: Harris	0	7	0	0	0.00

Extras	(1lb, 4w, 1nb, 0b)	6		
Total	10 Wkts, 101.4 overs	312		3.06 Runs/Over

Fall of wickets 1-1 (Cook, 1.3 ov), 2-20 (Carberry, 11.4 ov), 3-131 (Pietersen, 47.1 ov), 4-143 (Bell, 53.4 ov), 5-171 (Root, 64.2 ov), 6-210 (Stokes, 84.1 ov), 7-255 (Broad, 90.5 ov), 8-293 (Swann, 97.3 ov), 9-301 (Prior, 98.5 ov),10-312 (Panesar, 101.4 ov)

Bowling	O	M	R	W	Econ	SR	Extras
RJ Harris	19.4	3	54	3	2.74	39.3	(1nb, 2w)
MG Johnson	24	8	73	1	3.04	144	(2w)
PM Siddle	19	4	57	4	3.00	28.5	
NM Lyon	26	7	78	1	3.00	156	
SR Watson	6	3	6	0	1.00	–	
SPD Smith	7	0	43	1	6.14	42	

4

THE THIRD
TEST MATCH

Tuesday 10 December. Adelaide to Perth.

Today was our travel day, a three-hour Qantas flight
from Adelaide to Perth. I like everything about Perth
except the time it takes to fly here. Once we arrived, we
had a team recovery session before going our separate
ways to get ourselves ready for training tomorrow.

It's a light day, which had planned in con-
sideration of how short the turnaround is before the
Third Test match. The celebrations after Adelaide were
low-key. We had a team dinner, just a couple of beers,
and finished at about ten o'clock. I was quite tired from
the five days of play in Adelaide, where we really had
to grind out the win, so I went back to the hotel early to
get some sleep.

When I woke up this morning, I went to the gym for an early session to flush my legs out. The next three days are crucial for me to get the soreness out of my body and to clear my head for the massive game we have starting on Friday. This is the Ashes, if we win here. We have the precious commodity of momentum from Brisbane and Adelaide, and must be fully focused to keep a hold of it and not let England back in. As we have experienced before, once momentum shifts, the other side can get going and be hard to stop. So there is no room for complacency in our team, and I haven't seen any sign of it.

Wednesday 11 December. **Perth.**

After the unseasonal coolness of Adelaide, it's nice and hot here in Perth, 38 degrees Celsius with similar temperatures forecast through the week. If anything, it might get even hotter. While recovering from Adelaide and training for the Test match here, we are trying to make sure we are well prepared in terms of hydration and freshness.

Over the next two days, our training scheme is tailored to the specific demands of back-to-back Test matches. Practising on one of the two days is mandatory, but as individuals we can choose which of the two days we'll train. For my part, I'm doing both days. I trained this morning and will also go through my normal pre-Test match preparation session tomorrow. It's a personal choice, but for my part I like to stick to my proven routines.

I went into the nets this morning with the boys to get used to the bouncy Perth practice wickets, which are very different from Adelaide's drop-in deck. Footwork, timing, shot selection, and even how you adjust your eyes to the much brighter, whiter light here are all parts of the changes you have to make to this new environment. As usual with me, more work suits me rather than resting, and I enjoyed the session. The pace bowlers, who are taking things pretty easy, will also love it here.

Speaking of pace bowlers, our one concern going into the match is Ryan Harris, whose knee has swollen up a little bit. He'll do what he needs to get right, and we are confident that he will play. Nobody on earth could be more determined than Rhino. After his late start in international cricket, he had such a rough run with injuries between 2010 and 2013, he's now looking at the opportunity to play his seventh consecutive Test match and he is not going to let go of it. And we don't want him to! He has become such a vital bowler for us. While he hasn't so far dominated the wicket-taking here as much as he did in England, we all know that he, Sidds, Watto and Lyono have 'taken' the wickets at the other end for Mitch Johnson, that is, they have applied the pressure and followed the plans that have freed Mitch to bowl the way he has. It was very pleasing, though, to see Sidds and Rhino take wickets on their own account in that fourth innings in Adelaide.

Amid all these preparations, this week is a little different for me, as I will be playing my hundredth Test match for Australia. It's hard to put into words what that means. I think about my first match, back in 2004 in Bangalore, India, when I was so young and fresh and just went out there and batted with a clear head. I had my baggy green cap presented by Shane Warne, a hero from my childhood who turned into my teammate, my mentor and my friend. Our team, under Ricky Ponting and Adam Gilchrist, went on to win that series, which is still the only time Australia has won a Test series in India since 1969. It was an amazing experience, and the start of what has been a long nine and a half years of ups and downs. I still see the pivotal experience of my career, the most important thing that happened to me, as the moment in late 2005 when I was dropped from the Australian Test team. After an up-and-down series in England, when we lost the Ashes, I had made a poor start to the home series against the West Indies in 2005–06. Being dropped shaped me as a person because it hurt so badly that I changed my life and resolved, without any more compromises, to put cricket first. The pain of being dropped left me with a hunger that hasn't gone away.

The Australian Test team has had plenty of highs since then, but when we've had a rough trot, such as last year when we lost six Test matches in a row, it has brought me back to that essential source, the pain from which I have derived my motivation and my fight. I am not a big one for looking back over my career while I'm still playing (to be honest, I struggle to remember a lot of it!) but what I will never forget is the strength I drew from adversity.

Through all that, I have been given the privilege of taking on the Australian captaincy and have had to adjust to the added responsibility that that has placed on my batting. I have loved that part of the challenge.

At this moment, I am thinking of the many team-mates I have seen come and go during the nine and a half years I have been in the Test team. But most of all, I am thinking of the teammates I have with me here in Perth. The most special among them are guys who have played alongside me for the Australian team for so long. That said, every player in our current group is special to me in his own right. All I want, at this moment, is to win the Test match we are playing this week. If we don't, I can guarantee that my memories of my hundredth Test match will not be happy ones!

As part of the celebrations for this event, today I signed bats commemorating my hundredth Test. Channel Nine are selling memorabilia pieces, featuring bats signed by the previous eleven Australian cricketers to play 100 Test matches – Allan Border, David Boon, Steve Waugh, Mark Taylor, Ian Healy, Mark Waugh, Shane Warne, Glenn McGrath, Justin Langer,

Matthew Hayden, Ricky Ponting – and me. I can't really believe it. I guess it will sink in later.

Those signed bats are a memento for the public. Behind the scenes, there have been some other special moments. Today, a young boy, Jalen Smith, who is fighting a serious illness, came to meet me as part of the Make-A-Wish Foundation's program. Jalen and I spent an hour together before training. I took him around the WACA Ground, guided him through the changing room, and showed him where I sit. He went through all my bats and tried on my baggy green cap. I then showed him the wicket and spent some time with his family, playing some cricket on the outfield and signing some autographs. I hope I put a smile on Jalen's face. He is a dedicated cricket lover, a very nice young man, and I really feel for him in these tough times. To do something small, like give him an hour of my time, is the least I can do.

Thursday 12 December. **Perth.**

Our last day of preparation has been nice and hot again, and the boys got the practice they wanted personally. Everyone is in a good spot mentally and physically, with Rhino's knee looking like it will be fine. The one setback was that James Faulkner, who will be twelfth man again, got hit on the hand while facing Mitchell Johnson in the nets and broke his thumb. The X-ray showed a crack, which is disappointing for him. He won't be able to field. Nevertheless, he will stay with the group for the whole of the Test.

I took a look at the wicket, which appeared a bit green this morning before training, but by early afternoon, once it had had a bit of that baking Perth sun on it, it was much whiter and promises to be a good cricket wicket.

Most importantly, I can detect no complacency in the group. We've only won two Test matches all year. The whole country is talking about how well we are going and how we have demolished England in Brisbane and Adelaide, but we have longer memories than that. We know that just three weeks ago we were rank outsiders for this series. The pain from losing the winter series 3–0 in England is still raw, believe me. Our hunger to win more matches is intense. The boys are really looking forward to tomorrow.

Personally, I have had to refocus my attention back onto the game itself, after all the excitement around the event of my hundredth Test match. My family are flying over, which is nice, but aside from that I am trying to treat it as I would any Test match, with all my energy directed towards the team winning. And we all know what that means.

Friday 13 December. Perth.

Friday the 13th was looking a bit black for a while, but thanks to some excellent batting from Steve Smith,

Brad Haddin and Mitchell Johnson, we have made a fantastic comeback and feel we're in a strong position. Yet again, members of this team are playing for each other and showing a strong heart.

I have to acknowledge, first of all, the wonderful support I received for my hundredth Test match. It was a special day. Last night I received three unexpected gifts, from my mate and vice-captain Brad Haddin, from our fielding coach Mike Young, and from my beautiful wife Kyly. I also received a couple of cards with very moving messages from George Bailey, a true leader within our team, and our strength and conditioning coach Damien Mednis. These things go a long way. I have tried not to focus on the milestone at the expense of the Test, but sometimes I have to look up and just accept that it is a special day. When I looked into the stand today and saw my family sitting up there with Kyly, I knew where the heart of my support is.

Before the game, there was a presentation. Wally Edwards, the chairman of Cricket Australia, gave me a baggy green cap which was embroidered with my name and '100 Tests'. I shook hands with six of the eleven Australians who had played 100 Tests before me. Warnie was among them and, as well as it being great to see him as always, it's a kind of closing of the circle, as he gave me my baggy green for my first Test in Bangalore all those years ago.

This is also Alastair Cook's hundredth Test match, and it's an honour to share the occasion with such a fantastic cricketer. I will certainly never forget all those long hours in the field while he gave us such hell in 2010–11. He had also been presented with a special cap, but when we got together to shake hands, swap team sheets and toss the coin, we didn't acknowledge the moment in any particular way, both of us knowing that we had to put all of that behind us and get on with a crucial game of cricket.

I wasn't too bothered either way about the toss. This was a contrast to Adelaide, where I felt that winning the toss might give us a handy advantage. Here, I was reconciled in my head to losing it. I think I'm due to lose one anyway! But the wicket had a bit of life in it, and if we lost the toss I believed our bowlers could really shake up the England batting line-up this morning. Then again, we also knew that on another 38-degree day the sun and heat after lunch would flatten the wicket out and make it a good one to bat on.

Initially I thought I had lost the toss. For some reason, I thought I heard Alastair call 'Tails', and when it landed that way I expected to hear him say he was batting. But I was asked what I wanted to do, and I realised he must have called 'Heads'. For the third straight Test match, we were batting.

It was one of those mornings when the cricket seemed to be played at a rapid rate. Chris Rogers, who played on the WACA for many years, was middling everything, and raced to 11 runs off his first eight balls.

He might have been hitting it *too* well, because he pushed one off Stuart Broad wide of mid-on and called for the single. When they saw that it was going very fast to James Anderson, Chris and David Warner both stuttered before continuing. Anderson picked it up, turned and hit the wicket with a good throw, and Chris was out, frustratingly, as he had looked in fine touch.

Davey was in superb nick, and losing his opening partner did not slow him down. In the first six overs, he hit Broad straight down the ground and then through mid-wicket for fours off the front and back feet. He then took Anderson to the boundary twice, with a straight drive and another drive through cover. The fast wicket suits Davey, as we know after seeing his career-high 180 here against India two years ago.

Tim Bresnan got his chance here, coming into the England team for Monty Panesar, and he replaced Broad after three overs from the Prindiville Stand end. Shane Watson immediately dispatched him with a sweet cover drive. Anderson finished his spell from the Lillee–Marsh Stand end, and Broad came back in his place to try a different end. Straight away he got Watto, edging to slip after another confident start.

So I was out in the middle inside the first hour, which wasn't quite to plan but not totally unexpected on a first morning at the WACA. It is so different from everywhere else, playing here always takes some adjusting. All the same, I noticed that there was a bit less in the pitch for the bowlers than I had thought there would be when I inspected it this morning. My feet were moving all right, and England bowled fairly short to me. I got one away off the back foot from Broad, and then worked Bresnan through the field off the front foot. Davey was batting beautifully, and I sensed that if we got through this first session we could put on a big stand.

Ben Stokes came on for Bresnan, and struggled with his length at first. I hit a full toss for four past mid-off, and then cut one late through the gap in the slips cordon for another. Davey and I were going along fine until just before lunch. Bresnan came back on for Broad, switching to the Lillee–Marsh Stand end, and I was able to ease away a pull shot for four behind square leg.

Davey was backing himself, as always. He took a cheeky single off Stokes. We ran hard, and Kevin Pietersen's throw hit the stumps. Davey was in, but the ball bounced off and would have gone for four overthrows except that it smacked into umpire Marais Erasmus, which gave the crowd a laugh but robbed us of four runs!

Davey took his chances in an action-packed over from Bresnan just before lunch. He pulled a short one back down the wicket at hip-height. Bresnan stuck out his right hand but could not hold what would have been a great catch. He still grimaced in disappointment like he should have caught it. Davey then rubbed it in by cover-driving him for four and pulling him for six.

In the last over before lunch from the Lillee–Marsh Stand end, Graeme Swann was brought on to replace Bresnan. Davey got a single away. Then, with his first ball to me, Swann tossed it up. I got down the wicket and intended to drive it through extra-cover. But I wasn't quite to the pitch of the ball, and it spun across me and I only got it with the inside half of my bat. It flew to the on-side, just high enough for Cook to take a good diving catch at short mid-wicket. It was undoubtedly poor shot selection on my part, just when we were putting a solid stand together.

So I was back in the sheds, pretty disconsolate, for the lunch break, but Davey and Smithy made a bright start to the afternoon session. Smithy was getting down the wicket to Swann whenever he saw a chance, and although initially he wasn't able to pierce the field, he stuck to his plan, which was encouraging to see. As he was yet to make a score in this series, he probably felt under a little bit of pressure, but I don't think his place in the team would have been in any doubt just three matches since his big maiden Test hundred at the Oval. Still, he was expecting a lot of himself and worked his backside off yesterday and the day before at practice. This afternoon, after 15 scoreless balls, he kept using his feet, which requires some courage and skill, and he got off the mark by lofting Swann for a six over the bowler's head. He followed this with a delightful clip off his pads for four off Anderson, and you sensed that if he maintained concentration he was going to make a big one.

Davey also looked set for a hundred at least, going the aerial route a few times off Swann. When he was on 60, though, he went to cut Swann and sliced a catch to Michael Carberry at backward point.

George Bailey got off the mark quickly and then hit a sweet cover drive for four off Broad. Bresnan replaced Anderson at the Prindiville Stand end, and England set about a short-pitched attack. Broad bowled a succession of bouncers which George let pass over his head. Then he had a go at one, and top-edged it to deep backward square. We had now lost four quick wickets, and were five down for 143. If we weren't careful, we could be out in the field by this afternoon.

However, there was still Brad Haddin, who has not only batted with his usual style and attacking flair in this series, but has been 100 per cent dependable. England changed their plan of attack to him after he drove Bresnan beautifully through cover for four. For three or four overs, they went short-pitched. He had an element of luck, as we all need at these moments. He edged one just short of slips and a skied hook shot lobbed in the direction of fine leg but fell just short of the incoming fieldsman. He was hit on the glove, the ball popping up but landing before the slips fielders could get to it, and was also hit on the back. The ball leapt in the air, but just missed the stumps when it came down.

It was a tough period for Hadds, and he just had to stick it out. Meanwhile Smithy was blossoming. He got right over the top of the short ball, and pulled a number of boundaries in front of square leg off Stokes. He got down the wicket to Swann to drive another six. Between the attacking shots, he was leaving the ball with fine judgement. He did not play and miss once before getting to 50: error-free batting, which is a rare thing to see at this level on a first-day wicket. It was fantastic to see such a young player thinking things through, setting a plan and staying with it.

After 75 fighting minutes at the crease, Hadds finally broke out with a slog-sweep for six off Swann, and just before tea he hit a gorgeous cover drive off Bresnan for four. We had had a shaky start to that session, but when Smithy and Hadds came in for tea we were 5/220. That little battle had been the turning point in the day.

England began the evening session with Swann and Anderson bowling, but our boys were able to play them with a level of comfort and confidence that we were never quite able to attain in England. At home, with that little bit more experience under our belt, a growing sense of unity, and an enormous hunger to win, we have found the resources to fight and keep on fighting. Sometimes it feels like a well – you reach down and find something there, while at other times you don't. It's hard to explain. But the way I describe it is in the amount of *fight* we have in us. There are many variables that go into this, home conditions being one of them, but I honestly think that the change has been due to the amount of planning and thought we have put into our preparation, and the work we are prepared to do to execute in the middle. I can't speak for England, as I don't know what's going on inside their camp. But I know that in the Australian camp we have worked day and night to turn things around. To see Hadds and Smithy take on Anderson and Swann as they did this afternoon was a reward in itself.

Hadds kicked off the session with a lovely back-foot cover drive off Anderson. The English pace bowlers were still targeting Smithy with the short ball, but he just saw every one as another chance to score. He pulled Anderson away for four. Then Swann floated one up, and Smithy was like a cat, down the wicket, driving along the ground through the off-side field. When Swann lost his line, Smithy took advantage of a gap behind square leg and swept him fine. Meanwhile, Bresnan tested Hadds with a slower ball, an off-cutter, and Hadds saw it early before belting it straight back over his head and over the boundary. It wasn't risk-free batting – Hadds lofted one pull shot that landed short of Michael Carberry running in from mid-wicket – but it was beautiful to watch, really aggressive and full of purpose.

The breakthrough came, as so often, after a period of sustained pressure. Broad and Stokes managed to stop the scoring for a few overs, and then Hadds miscued a pull shot and was caught by Anderson off Stokes. He was disappointed to get out after doing so much hard work, but what a recovery it was – he and Smithy had almost doubled our score in little more than two hours. We had gone from the chance of a sub-200 score to the possibility of 400. Hadds and Smithy deserve all the credit for that.

Mitch Johnson went out to face the second new ball, and was in the kind of form we saw from him in Brisbane. He is another player who enjoys the ball coming onto the bat, and he smashed some quick runs, no doubt disheartening the English who would have been hoping for another breakthrough with the new ball. Smithy, at the other end, went on to notch his hundred, a great individual milestone and a special moment for the team in the changing room. We are 6/326 at the end of the day, having turned an awkward position into a strong one. Those runs Smithy, Hadds and Mitch made in the second half of the day could be the decisive factor by the end of this Test match. We will be hoping to scratch out a few more in the morning and to get past 400, which is the kind of sound platform you need when you have to go out to bowl and field in extreme heat.

Saturday 14 December. Perth.

Not a bad day for us. It has been an interesting passage of Test cricket, and I would say that the match is evenly poised, with us having the slight upper hand due to the runs we have on the board. Some crucial wickets late in the day also helped. But we are a long, long way from finishing the job.

Our tail scratched and clawed their way to 385. It was a pretty good outcome, but I am greedy for runs and was hoping we might back it into 400. To their credit, England bowled well this morning. Broad started with a good pitched-up ball to Mitch Johnson, cutting short what had promised to be a spectacular innings. Then Smithy survived a caught-behind appeal from a suspected inside edge off the bowling of Anderson. England referred it to the DRS, and the new real-time Snickometer suggested a noise. The decision was, to Smithy's dismay, overturned by the third umpire.

We had lost our two overnight batsmen quickly, but to the great credit of Peter Siddle, Ryan Harris and Nathan Lyon, the last two wickets put on a very handy 47 runs. Having recovered from 5/143 to a total of 385, I can't be disappointed.

We had just shy of half an hour to bowl at Alastair Cook and Michael Carberry before breaking for lunch, and did not enjoy a lot of luck in that little period. Rhino, bowling from the Prindiville Stand end, got a leading edge from Cook that flew to Smithy's left at third slip. Smithy made a good attempt at it but just failed to pull it in. A couple of overs later, I brought Shane Watson on for Mitch from the Lillee–Marsh Stand end, and he had Cook playing an almost identical shot, again edging at catchable height but just between third slip and gully.

In the hour after lunch, we probably didn't put in our best bowling spell. Cook and Carberry were intent on rotating the strike as much as possible, and were largely able to do so. We struggled to find the right WACA length. We didn't overdo the short ball, which is always a false temptation here – 90 per cent of wickets fall to balls well pitched up – but it just took some time for us to find the length that could tie the batsmen down.

All the same, we were continuing to strive to create chances. Carberry nicked one off Mitch that bisected the gap between myself and Smithy in slips. Then Carberry top-edged a pull off Sidds, which somehow landed in between Hadds, square leg and fine leg, all converging on the ball at the same time. Between those chances, the two English left-handers played some confident attacking strokes and got to the mid-afternoon drinks break at no wicket for 72.

Soon afterwards, Rhino came on at the Prindiville Stand end to replace Sidds, and we decided to change the angle and come around the wicket. Carberry likes leaving the ball close to his off stump, and we have felt that something angling in to him might cause a little bit of uncertainty. Sure enough, Rhino bowled the perfect delivery, and Carberry went to play at it before pulling his bat away. As he withdrew his bat, the ball rose and cannoned off his inside edge down onto the stumps. It might be seen as an unlucky dismissal, as the ball could have ricocheted out of harm's way, but from our point of view it was anything but a matter of chance: it was the result of careful observation, conversations in the field, a change of angle, and perfect execution by the bowler.

That breakthrough changed the whole tenor of the afternoon. Cook and Carberry had been going along pretty smoothly, but now Nathan Lyon was really troubling Cook, who was playing and missing and edging and finding it hard to get off strike. I brought Watto on for Rhino from the Prindiville Stand end, and he immediately got some swing with the ageing ball. Joe Root, who stood in our path for so long just the other day in Adelaide, played forward and nicked one to Hadds. He referred it to the DRS, but the replay confirmed the umpire's decision and we had our second wicket.

Now Cook and Pietersen were the obstacles. We have had good success against these two this year in both England and Australia, but with such fantastic records they would be confident that they can make big scores, and maybe this would be their day. Pietersen looked in good touch, but we concentrated on bowling a very dry line and building the pressure so that each bowler could target the guy he wanted to be bowling to.

Cook had scored quite freely in the first hour after lunch, but after drinks we managed to dry him up. He had got to 35 in 55 balls, but off his next 70 balls he was only able to score ten runs. Pietersen, meanwhile, only scored four runs off his first 44 balls, which was very unlike Kevin. In partnership, they went through 11 overs scoring only 18 runs as our seamers bowled with fantastic discipline. It was a battle of patience out there, and I was quietly pleased to see that our guys were not wilting. Sidds bowled especially well at Cook, having him playing and missing repeatedly, while Rhino troubled Pietersen with a play and miss and then a nick that fell just short of slips.

It was an outstanding period of tight bowling, but as the afternoon wore on I got the feeling that without wickets our guys were going a bit quiet. It was extremely hot, too. Bowlers and batsmen both suffer in the heat, and sometimes the heat turns cricket into a contest to prove that your concentration can hold up longer than the other guy's. But we needed some help, so when I brought Mitch back on at the Lillee–Marsh Stand end, I waved to the crowd to make a bit of noise and get up his backside. They responded straight away. The mood changed, and I have to thank the crowd for getting involved and turning up the heat on the batsmen. When cricketers talk about the benefits of playing at home – and the results on the international stage certainly suggest the relative advantage of home soil – crowd support is one of the major, if underestimated, factors. It is only in a home Test that you can turn to the stands and rev up the spectators and obtain from them the kind of buzz that can change the way the players are feeling in the middle.

Mitch bowled a good bouncer at Pietersen, which got everyone even more excited, and I brought on Nathan Lyon from the Prindiville Stand end. Cook cut him for four, but we didn't mind this. Nathan got him out on the cut shot in Brisbane, and with the increased bounce and pace in the Perth wicket, the cut can be a dangerous stroke to play off a finger-spinner. Next ball, Nathan put it in much the same place, a fraction fuller, and Cook mishit his cut. He had been tied down for so long, he must have been wanting to score runs, and he sliced his cut to David Warner at backward point.

This, along with the noise the crowd had started making, was the mood-changer. Mitch bowled a fiery over at Pietersen. There was an edge through slips and a skied pull shot only just over mid-wicket. The temperature was right up. I brought Sidds on for Mitch, and straight away he got Pietersen out yet again. He bowled one that was not quite short enough to pull, and Pietersen cross-batted it towards mid-on. For a moment the ball looked like it was going to clear Mitch, but the big fellow, running back, showed all his athleticism and skill to hurl himself into the air and take the catch overhead. Great bowling, great catch, and full credit to the Perth crowd!

We didn't take another wicket this afternoon, as Ian Bell and Ben Stokes consolidated through to stumps. Tomorrow morning, we will have 12 overs left to bowl with the old ball, and we really want to capitalise and get a breakthrough before the new ball falls due, so that the lower order will be exposed to some pace bowling with a shiny new rock. All up, we didn't have a lot of luck today. I hope the hard work in building the pressure will deliver those edges and chances tomorrow that we just missed today. With the heat due to build again, it will be crucial to start the day well and get our bowlers back into the cool of the changing room.

Sunday 15 December. Perth.

We were relying on our bowlers to get us a first-innings lead, and they delivered again. Everything I could have asked of them, they did, and more. We have had a brilliant day of Test cricket and have put ourselves in the box seat for this Test match.

I thought last night that it was imperative to get a breakthrough in the 12 overs we still had with the old ball. Either we would have two recognised batsmen, Ian Bell and Ben Stokes, at the wicket and settled in when the new ball fell due, or we would have their lower order exposed.

Bell and Stokes started confidently enough on a day that was even hotter than the past few. The Fremantle Doctor hasn't arrived in the afternoon to give us any relief, though a mild breeze has sprung up late each day. The mornings, on the other hand, have been very hot,

even brutal, with the temperature topping 50 degrees
Celsius out in the middle.

Ryan Harris only waited for his ninth ball of the day
to duck one in on Bell. Umpire Erasmus turned down our
appeal. He might have thought, as I did, that Bell nicked the
ball onto his pad. Rhino came down the wicket and was
absolutely adamant that Bell had not hit it. Brad Haddin, to
whom I would usually look for the final verdict on whether
to challenge an umpire's decision, was unsure. I looked at
the scoreboard and saw that we only had nine overs to go
before we would replenish our stock of two DRS referrals.
So it seemed wise to have a crack, even if I was less than
confident about getting the decision overturned. I know
that there is a lot of talk about the purpose of the DRS
being to remove 'howlers' from the game, and Marais
Erasmus's decision in this case certainly wasn't a poor one.
But, on the other hand, my role as captain during a Test
match is not to think about philosophical questions on the
purpose of the DRS. My job is to make decisions, within
the laws and the spirit of the game, that will help us win a
match. So even though it was a bit of a speculator, I have
no regrets about asking for the referral.

It turned out that the bowler, Rhino, was right! The
replay showed no contact of ball with bat, and the ball
hitting the stumps. Bell was given out, and Matt Prior
was in.

By now it was stinking hot, which is a test for
bowlers and fielders, but also, perhaps less obviously,

for batsmen. The hot sunlight on the pitch had had an effect too, with big cracks opening up in different parts of the wicket, but most distractingly in a wobbly line in front of the batsman at each end.

We have found over the years in Perth that the effect of these cracks is mental more than anything. When the ball hits a crack, it tends to deviate so much that it is not actually going to get a batsman out. But the thing is, the batsman can't know that for sure. Their instincts say cracks are dangerous. So it is only natural that those cracks will create doubts in visiting batsmen's heads, particularly if they haven't played a lot in these conditions. Three overs after Bell was out, Mitch bowled one from the Lillee–Marsh Stand end to Stokes and it pretty much went sideways. Of course, it was no threat of getting him out, but all the same Stokes must have wondered what was going to happen next. The following ball did not hit a crack, but he played a slightly unsure forward push and nicked it to Hadds. That's what I mean by a mental effect. The ball that did *not* hit the crack was the dangerous one, but the scene was set by the ball that deviated.

Prior followed soon after, under-edging an attempted pull shot off Peter Siddle, and we had taken three wickets with the old ball, about as good as we had hoped for. I was really keen on getting a single breakthrough before the second new ball, but now we had three. It was magic, in those conditions, for the bowlers to come up with the goods yet again. I was bowling them in very short spells, usually three overs, or four at the most. I did not ask them if they were happy with short spells or not. Bowlers sometimes want more time to apply pressure, and some of them prefer not to feel the onus to take a wicket in a very short spell. But to their credit, the members of our bowling cartel have accepted their roles and gone along with whatever I have asked of them.

Shane Watson was bowling the 81st over from the Prindiville Stand end, and after Tim Bresnan drove him for four he took the new ball. It only took a few balls from Mitch at the Lillee–Marsh Stand end to bring another wicket. Stuart Broad played back to a yorker, and was hit on the foot. He was plumb LBW, and as it turned out it was a double blow, because the ball hurt his foot so badly that he had to go to hospital for an X-ray. The news is that it's not a break, only bruising, but later today he was not able to come out and bowl or field. That surprised us. In fact, we could not believe it. We thought that only a broken bone could have kept him off the field.

Sidds and Rhino picked up the last two wickets, so overall the spoils were shared around. Any of the five bowlers could have picked up five or six wickets in this innings, they did so well putting the ball in the dangerous areas, but it was nice to see everyone getting some reward. Whatever vestiges of juice were remaining in that wicket, our bowlers got the most out of them. They deserve the credit for our 134-run first-innings lead.

Nothing specific was said in the changing room during the innings break, just a few general words about playing with positive intent. You never need to tell David Warner to play like that. He will back himself in any situation. Chris Rogers was outstanding too, clipping some attractive on-drives off his pads. In Graeme Swann's first over, Davey charged down the wicket and missed, and fortunately for us Matt Prior missed the stumping. Then Chris, when he was on 26, nicked Anderson. In a very similar scenario to when we dropped Joe Root at Lord's in July, neither the keeper nor the first slip, Alastair Cook, moved towards the ball as it flew between them. Cook stuck out his right hand at the last moment but grassed the chance. It was tough for England, and I know how they feel.

Our openers got us to none for 123 at tea, a commanding position in the game. Chris was driving beautifully, both straight and through the on-side, while Davey was playing all the shots in his wide repertoire. It can look easy when batsmen are on top, but it required great courage for them to play so attackingly on a wicket that was not consistent. Stokes got one to jump up and hit Chris in the ribs, and Davey was missed again on 89, when Prior again failed to stump him.

With the score on 157, nearly a 200-run lead for us, Bucky lost his wicket, caught off Bresnan, for a valuable half-century. Watto went out there and played with care, unleashing a couple of booming cover drives but for the most part treating the bowling and the conditions with respect. Davey got to his century, his second for the series, which made me very happy, having declared on him so close to his hundred in Adelaide. He took that decision with good grace, and maybe it was karma that he got the three figures this time.

He was out about an hour before stumps, skying one off Swann, before Watto and I set about consolidating and building our stronghold. I think we are far enough ahead in the game to be dictating terms, but that can quickly change if you are careless and throw away cheap second-innings wickets. Cook shuffled his bowlers around, and the game was quite tense. I have to say, it is hard not to think about or look at those gaping black cracks in the pitch when you're taking strike. They are in your mind, because you think that if you go onto the front foot, any ball can potentially duck sideways or leap up and hit you in the face. The ball wasn't actually doing that much, but I found it a testing psychological game. Watto played with a broad bat, as always, and I was in awe of one on-drive he crashed off Anderson. It was fantastic batting.

I had high hopes of being out in the middle tomorrow morning, but seven overs before stumps I was beaten and bowled by a pretty good ball from Stokes that nipped off the wicket. Watto and Steve Smith saw us through to stumps, and to say I am extremely pleased with where we're at is an understatement. Our position is a credit to the whole team. Tomorrow morning, my only thoughts are on how long to bat for. I'm thinking that another 100 runs will take our lead to about 470, which should be enough, and will leave us five sessions to bowl England out and bring the urn back to where it belongs.

Socialising during a Test match is not usually part of my agenda, but tonight I went to the Crown Metropol at Burswood to have a quiet dinner with Kyly and Shane Warne, just the three of us. Warnie wanted to take me out to congratulate me on my hundredth Test match. Kyly was very understanding and patient as Shane and I spoke a lot about the position our team is in and how the Test match might develop. As always, Shane was honest with me, giving constructive feedback about the team's performance and what he has seen through the series. He is complimentary to all the players, every one of them. His positive attitude always makes him a pleasure to be with, and it was a really nice dinner.

For me personally, it was very special to acknowledge what Kyly and Shane have done to get me to this point. Without those two, I certainly would not be sitting where I am today. I have played with some great players who have given me a lot of support through the years, but none has been more important than Shane. And Kyly has changed my life off the field. To have her on tour with me this year, in England and in Australia, has been a great joy and has helped me in countless ways, whether things are going well or the opposite. The big moment, taking back the Ashes, feels so close now, I can barely contain my excitement. But at dinner, it was not about discussing how good that's going to feel; it was more about sharing the pleasure I have taken in the team's performance with my great friend and my wife.

Monday 16 December. Perth.

We are so close! But not there yet. Every time I think of how tantalisingly close we are to winning back the Ashes, I remind myself that we have work to do, maybe a lot of work, and that we can take nothing for granted until the final ball is bowled.

Today was a fantastic day, again. These past three Test matches have been out of this world. I almost can't believe how everything this team stands for and tries to do has come together in these 13 days of Ashes cricket. But this is precisely what we have planned, so I guess there is nothing unbelievable about it at all.

At the start of play, I asked the remaining batsmen to make 100 runs as quickly as they could, without throwing their wickets away unnecessarily or attempting what they couldn't do. I had a clear plan to get the lead out to 470 and put the English openers in for a 20-minute session before lunch. It is common sense that batting is hardest when you are starting your innings, so putting

Alastair Cook and Michael Carberry in for little mini-sessions like this, when they will have to start yet again after lunch, felt like a bonus, doubling our chances of attacking them when they were still adjusting to being in the middle.

Our middle-order batsmen could not have answered my request better. In fact, they exceeded all expectations. Steve Smith didn't last long, but Shane Watson went on an absolute rampage, ripping the bowling apart as he does so often in short-form cricket. From the first over of the day he went after Graeme Swann, driving him time and again over the mid-on and mid-off boundaries. It was incredible, not only for the result he achieved, though that was considerable, but for the psychological effect on both teams. What also pleased me was how Shane and George Bailey clearly put the team ahead of themselves.

Both of those batsmen have been under different kinds of pressure. Watto has been an integral part of our team with his batting, fielding, bowling and leadership throughout the away and home legs of these two Ashes series. Today, he answered emphatically the pressure to score a hundred. He only gave one chance, and it wasn't a chance really. On 90, he hit yet another towering off-drive off James Anderson. We didn't know if Tim Bresnan, positioning himself on the rope, would be under the ball, or if it was going too far. As it happened, Bresnan took a really good catch over his head, but the momentum of the ball's flight was such that it took

Bresnan over the boundary with it. Six! Three balls later, Watto tucked Anderson away behind fine leg to bring up the three figures. Whatever pressure he was under, he had responded in the best possible style.

He was out a few minutes later, in circumstances that I have to report but which weren't flattering to anybody. Watto tried to hit Bresnan out of the ground, but only succeeded in sending the ball straight up in the air. Ian Bell came in from cover to accept the catch halfway down the wicket. The ball was up there so long, Watto could just about have run two. But he was so down on himself for throwing away the chance to make more runs that he just walked off to the side. Bell, meanwhile, dropped the ball. Watto had still only moved to the side of the crease, and George was yelling at him to run. Bell didn't even see what was going on. He was so upset about dropping the catch that he turned his back on the ball and was walking towards his fielding position. Watto and George scampered for their single, and Bresnan picked the ball up. He probably could have run to the wicket and removed the bails, but he was so stirred up at not getting the wicket, he just pegged the ball at the stumps. He hit – only just – and Watto was out. I guess everyone who saw it will remember it. It wasn't the greatest piece of cricket anyone has seen. But if they saw that, they would also have seen Watto's hitting over the previous hour, which was truly awesome and will stick in the memory for a long time to come.

George had a different kind of tension to deal with. He is only playing his third Test match, and I can remember how at that stage of your career everything is new and you feel under constant scrutiny. Today he came in just as England took the second new ball. Anderson and Ben Stokes were bowling, and the pitch was misbehaving whenever the ball hit a crack. For George, there was every motivation to play for himself, just try and get a not-out and secure his place for another Test match. Instead, he went on a tear every bit as destructive as Watto's. George was only eight when Watto got out. He then had a let-off, skying Bresnan to cover, where Anderson and Bell became confused about who was catching it, and both let it fall to the ground. Then Brad Haddin got out, characteristically throwing caution to the wind in the chase for quick runs for the team, and George was still only ten. We had just passed our target of 100 runs in the session, so George knew he would only have a few more minutes. At the fall of Hadds's wicket, I sent the new batsman, Mitch Johnson, out with a message: two more overs, and I was declaring.

What happened in Anderson's next over will go down in the history books. The first ball was short and outside the off stump, and George made a beautiful late adjustment to flick it over the slips cordon for four. The second ball was a good one, straight at the stumps, and George just smacked it over the bowler's head and over the sightscreen for one of the cleanest sixes you will ever see.

128

To the third ball, an attempted yorker, he stepped across to the off-side and clipped it off his pads for two. The fourth was also on the stumps, a little shorter, and George again stepped across to the off-side and lifted it over the infield for a four to the square leg boundary. Ball five, a half-volley on the off stump, he drove sweetly all the way over the mid-off boundary, clearing Bresnan. And the last ball, which Anderson again had right on the stumps, George got under and carted over long-on for another six. You would not have said any of it was bad bowling, but George had taken 28 runs off the over, equalling a world record set by Brian Lara. The best thing about it, for me? George could have got himself out any ball. He was taking risks. He would have walked off with a score that might possibly put pressure on his place in the team. And he didn't care. He just went out to try to load up our lead as heavily as possible and demoralise the opposition. I was so proud of him and Watto. When I called George and Mitch in at the end of that over, all of the boys were on a terrific high.

We now had a cushion of 503 runs, a handy 30 more than I had accounted for this morning. Out in the field, I gave Ryan Harris the first over with the new ball, as usual, and he picked the Prindiville Stand end. England had about half an hour to bat until lunch. One wicket would be brilliant . . . and we got it first ball. Rhino bowled one similar to a number of balls he bowled on the tour of England, swinging a little, pitching on an in-between length, and hitting the top of off stump. It was pretty much unplayable. I would say it is the ball of the series so far – maybe the ball of the century, seeing this one is only 13 years old! No player wants to get a peach like that, a perfect delivery, least of all on the first ball of the innings. Still, I wasn't sympathising with Alastair Cook at the time. I was just thrilled for Rhino that he bowled such a ball in such a situation. It clipped the bails and we were delirious. The player who, more than any other Englishman, has shown the capacity to bat for very long periods in a match-saving mode was out of the picture. A perfect start. Nine to go!

We soon thought we had another. Just before lunch, Mitch bowled a very good ball to the new batsman, Joe Root, trapping him in front. Our big appeal was turned down by the on-field umpire. We might have been a bit over-excited with the roll we were on, and, after a bit of a discussion with Hadds, I decided to refer it. The DRS replay showed that the ball had pitched outside leg stump, so even though it would have hit the stumps it could not be given out. It was not a great decision of mine to refer it, and we were down to one remaining referral in the first 80 overs. I hoped my error wouldn't come back to haunt us.

Still, we were in great spirits at lunch, and were confident that we could keep our momentum rolling. I was trying not to think about the Ashes, but it was hard. The minute you let those thoughts take hold, however, is when you make a mistake. So I stayed in the moment even more than usual, making a special effort not to get ahead of myself. Soon after the break, I brought Nathan Lyon on from the Lillee–Marsh Stand end, where he hasn't done much of his bowling, but a breeze had sprung up from the south that he could bowl into and possibly gain some drift. He had Michael Carberry in some bother, with an attempted drive flying over slip. Overall, though, Carberry was batting well once again, and Root was digging in. They had added more than 60 runs when I brought Shane Watson on from the Prindiville Stand end in place of Peter Siddle. Watto bowled five balls to Carberry, and then decided to switch his angle to round the wicket. He swung his first ball in, Carberry missed it, and we all went up for the LBW appeal, to which the umpire raised his finger. Carberry must have known it was out, and did not ask for a referral.

Every wicket would be hard to prise out. We set ourselves for a long fight. When Kevin Pietersen came in, he got off the mark with a fine straight drive off Watto. At the drinks break we told ourselves to stick to our plans, and for a while we did, pinning down Root until he got frustrated enough to attempt to drive a wide, full ball from Mitch Johnson. His bat hit the ground, but we also thought he nicked it, and Hadds took an athletic catch diving to his right. The umpire agreed with us, giving Root out. The batsman, deceived by the contact between his bat and the turf, referred the decision without consulting Pietersen, and the replay showed clearly that he was out. You beauty. Seven to go!

But we still had arguably England's two best batsmen ahead of us. Pietersen and Bell were clearly determined to stop the rot and take some runs off us, shifting the pressure back our way. Mitch bowled extremely well to both of them, cutting Bell in half with a short one and getting Pietersen flicking off an inside edge down the leg-side, where the ball flew just out of reach of Hadds's spectacular leap. Still, we could not get the wicket in that session, and England went to tea three down.

Just before the break, I had Nathan Lyon bowling from the Lillee–Marsh Stand end. Pietersen was looking to get after him. We always have a deep mid-on for Pietersen facing Lyono, in case he miscues a booming drive, but before tea I brought the man up to an orthodox mid-on to tempt Pietersen to try to hit over the top. He went for it, and was evidently bullish about attacking Nathan.

After tea, I was happy for Pietersen to keep playing that shot. He lofted Lyono over the fence, but our plan was to keep on tossing them up in the hope that he would make an error of judgement. Immediately after the six, the moment came: he went for another, didn't quite get it in the middle, and we held our breaths. It seemed to hang in the air forever as Ryan Harris positioned himself under it. Better him than me. Down it came, down, down . . . and he pouched it. At first he was so still, curling up on the ground in relief, that it was not clear whether he had caught or dropped it. But when he got up, clutching the ball and grinning ear to ear, we were jubilant. I thought it was terrifically courageous bowling from Nathan Lyon to subject himself to punishment in the hope of getting that big wicket.

In the next hour, things swung back England's way as Bell and Ben Stokes put on a half-century partnership at a run a minute. We did not bowl all that badly, but we were getting excited by the cracks. Mitch bowled one to Stokes that jagged at what looked like a right angle, and Watto bowled one to Bell that ran along the ground. Our eyes bulged as we saw the potential of the cracks, and we made the mistake of aiming at them, hoping for them to do the work, rather than sticking to our plans. We incorrectly perceived the cracks to be a bigger weapon than they were. So far in the match, the cracks have been responsible for some weird and wonderful things, but not one wicket has fallen to a ball that hit a crack. Most of the time they deviate too far to seriously trouble the batsmen. So we fell into a bit of a trap there. We knew the cracks weren't going to take wickets for us, but instinct took over and we couldn't help ourselves.

After the last drinks break, Watto and Sidds went back to basics and aimed to bowl a dry spell. Eventually it worked. Sidds bowled a short one to Bell outside his off stump, and, being so strong behind point, he was confident enough to glide it over third slip for four. Cleverly, Sidds thought it was worth trying again, despite the risk of giving away runs. He did it, Bell tried the same shot, and we heard a clear nick as it went through to Hadds. The umpire gave it not out, but it took me no time to ask for a referral. Sure enough, our appeal was confirmed, and Bell was on his way – and out of our way.

Stokes and Prior got through to stumps, adding another 31. Stokes is unbeaten on 72 tonight, after playing well and taking advantage of what I thought was some inconsistent bowling. There have not been many sessions when our bowling has been less than optimal, but this was one. We sat down and had a chat after stumps, and sorted things out. We know what to do tomorrow.

So, it's not over yet. Five wickets to go, starting with two good players in Stokes and Prior. Below them, Tim Bresnan, Graeme Swann and Stuart Broad have all made plenty of runs in Test cricket. They are not to be underestimated. The morning will be a big one. We will have 13 overs, or about an hour, before the second new ball falls due. As with day two, we plan to break through with the old ball and expose the tail-enders to the new one. It's going to be a big, big day.

Tuesday 17 December. **Perth. Morning.**

It's five o'clock in the morning. I am wide awake and getting my stuff organised in my hotel room. I haven't been able to sleep.

There are a lot of different feelings swirling around inside me. The excitement around potentially winning the Ashes today is hard to control. I think that's the main thing that is stopping me from sleeping. We have put so much into this, for so long, and success is so close, I am struggling to stay calm.

No doubt there is also the fear of losing. England still have to make 250 runs, which is a lot with five wickets in hand, but there is a chance they can win the game. Stokes looks like a capable young batsman who is taking every day as it comes. Last year, Faf du Plessis came in for his first Test match in Adelaide and played a miracle innings to stop us from winning. It can happen when you are young and enjoying Test cricket for what it is, nothing but a game, and your mind is clear. Which makes Stokes a real danger.

With Stokes is Matt Prior, who averages more than 40 in Test cricket. Even though he hasn't had a great year against us with the bat, we all know how good he is. Is he due? Earlier this year he found himself in this same position against New Zealand, and he batted through the fifth day to save the match.

I am not sure if it's fear, as such, that is at the front of my mind. I have to find another name for it. What it is, is respect for cricket. Cricket is a game that is capable of producing the unexpected. It isn't like rugby league or Australian rules football, where a game can be pretty much over by half-time because one team is so far ahead. In cricket, until the last run is scored or the last wicket is taken, anything can still happen. We have to go out there today with respect for England's chances, and not treat it as if the game owes us a victory. We have to work for it, and overcome a dogged opponent. Every run counts! We have to play cricket, not just sit back and expect everything to come to us.

So it's that mixture of apprehension and anticipation that I am feeling. I'm thinking a lot about the possibility that we will win the Ashes today, and what that will mean for us. I guess that is the source of the excitement that I am trying to keep at bay. One thing I will say to the players today is that individually every man in that room has been through a lot in his career, no matter where each one is now. For all the diverse journeys we have taken to get here, the highs and lows of life and cricket have put us in this position, the eleven of us, here and now. That experience of life in cricket is what we run on. Cricket is a team sport, but the individual sacrifices and dedication, what you put into the game, give you the reward. That's what today is about. We want to make it special for every player and for our families, friends, wives, partners, kids and fans. So many people have shown us support in tough times, and I think about them every day. I know that today can be as special for them as it is for us. That includes our support staff, who do so much behind the scenes to get us onto the field each day in the right frame of mind.

Leadership can be about converting negatives into positive energy. Hardship becomes our fuel. Hatred of losing fuels our respect for the game. The criticism we have borne can increase our drive to prove ourselves. I don't think the media, be they journalists or past players, have fairly represented what Australian fans think of us over the past year. But I thank those who have criticised us, because it gives us the drive and hunger to succeed.

An exciting morning, then, and a nervous one. I know the boys will be up for this occasion.

Tuesday 17 December. Perth. Evening.

Yes! It's the end of the Test match. The urn is coming home.

I can't describe how I am feeling now. These were three amazing victories, and there is a feeling around this group that I have not experienced in 100 Test matches. I said as much before the series, but it has taken the team's achievements on the field to prove that what I was seeing was more than just what I was hoping to see. They have worked unbelievably hard, and this is their reward.

The smiles on the boys' faces as we took the last wicket today will be imprinted on my memory forever.

Yes!

To go back to the beginning. As I recorded in my diary this morning, it was a restless night for me, and I gathered it was similar for pretty much everyone else in the playing and support group. We got to the ground filled with this same apprehension, the tension between excitement on the one hand and respect for England's hopes on the other. I said to the team before play, 'I know there's a few nerves in here, but we are in this position due to skill, not emotion, and if we keep relying on our skill we will get the result.'

The morning session was challenging. Mitchell Johnson started from the Lillee–Marsh Stand end, and got one to cut back and go through Ben Stokes in the first over. No wicket, though. Mitch also troubled Matt Prior with some steepling bouncers, but Prior got out of the way.

Ryan Harris took the ball from the Prindiville Stand end, and he also had his moments. In his second over he had an LBW appeal against Stokes turned down, and then he had Stokes playing and missing. In Rhino's third over, he hit a crack and the ball jagged so far that Stokes missed it by half a metre. We were all laughing grimly. The cracks do too much. But they can unsettle the batsman, and immediately after that incident Stokes inside-edged one, and played and missed another, but then hit a solid on-drive for the first four of the day.

After Mitch had bowled three overs, Peter Siddle came on and replaced him. Prior defended him soundly, but then played and missed at the last ball of Sidds's first over.

In his second over, Sidds got one to shoot off a crack and hit Stokes on his pad, but it pitched outside leg and was missing the leg stump. The near-misses were mounting up. Were England growing confident that this might be their day? We certainly felt that so many balls were deviating and so many shots were being attempted and missed, something was bound to go our way. But when?

Shane Watson replaced Ryan after a four-over spell, but again the breakthrough refused to come. After 13 overs, I took the second new ball and brought back Ryan and Mitch. With the very first delivery, Ryan got the ball to hit a crack and miss both Stokes's outside edge and the off stump. The batsmen then took a streaky single, but we couldn't pull off the run-out. Then Stokes played and missed the sixth ball of an action-packed first over with the second new ball. Nevertheless, England survived.

By drinks, they had got to 5/283. They would have been thinking, we have survived one hour, only five to go. On the other hand, we were thinking, something *has to* break.

After drinks, Prior began to score more freely, getting Ryan away through slips and then off his pads for a pair of boundaries. He hooked Ryan in the air and it dollied above square leg, but fell to ground before George Bailey could get in from deep square. Then Mitch bowled a searing bouncer that nipped off a crack and beat Hadds to run off for four byes. All the luck was going England's way, and the score was creeping towards 300.

Finally, Mitch got the wicket, not with an especially good ball, but it was due reward for all the good ones that had unluckily missed the edge. He bowled a wide half-volley that Prior chased and edged to Brad Haddin. We felt a great lifting of pressure. With Tim Bresnan coming in, we only had the bowlers to remove. But no – we had to remember that Bresnan is an accomplished lower-order batsman, so we had to keep on working. No wicket was going to come easily.

Stokes was getting near his hundred, his first in Test cricket, so we hoped we could capitalise on the nerves he would be feeling. On 94, he played a pull shot off Mitch that ballooned into the air but ran away to the boundary. Then he hit a nicely timed straight drive that he probably thought would bring up his hundred, but Mitch deflected it into umpire Erasmus, who could not get out of the way. Mitch bowled another bouncer, and Stokes took the bait. It hit his glove, but lobbed out of Hadds's reach and ran away to fine leg. That was his hundred. Well played. Then, with the adrenalin flowing, he chased one outside off and flashed it over slips for another four.

In the circumstances, it was a very good hundred. He is only playing his second Test match, he's under enormous pressure from the bowling, he's playing on a wicket riddled with cracks, and he has made a century he will remember all his life. I expect it will be the first of many.

The runs were coming fast now, too fast for our comfort, and I brought Sidds back on from the Lillee–Marsh Stand end. For the first time today, I introduced spin, Nathan Lyon replacing Ryan Harris at the Prindiville Stand end. Stokes took him on, coming down the wicket and lofting a six and then again, later in the over, driving a four down the ground. Bresnan cut Sidds for another boundary, and another ball deviated wildly off a crack and ran away for four byes. England had their required runs down below 180. This match was not going to end in a draw. Just before lunch, we almost had Stokes out when he popped an inside edge at catchable height off Nathan Lyon, but it landed just clear of Steve Smith's dive. Close, but he was still there.

So we went into the changing rooms to the noisy cheering of the English fans. England were 6/332, having lost 1/82 in the session. They needed another 172 to win, and we still needed four wickets.

During the lunch break, the changing room was pretty quiet. I grabbed some food and sat alone in my cubicle. I was not too concerned about having only taken one wicket. The wickets would come if we kept bowling as we had been. I just sat there quietly and ran our plans through my mind, staying clear, staying focused.

Just before we went out, I said to the boys, 'Let's go and win a Test match.'

The sun was still beating down, though it was a fraction cooler than the past few days. Maybe it was in the mid-thirties. The bowlers kept on running in and bowling in the right areas. After the way they have performed this year, I was very glad to be relying on these five guys.

We started with Nathan Lyon from the Prindiville Stand end and Mitch Johnson from the Lillee–Marsh Stand end. The action started immediately, with Nathan bowling to the left-handed Stokes from around the wicket. He got one to slide back, and Stokes left it alone. The ball clipped his pad flap and might have been coming back in far enough to hit the stumps, but was not quite close enough to the off stump for us to appeal with any conviction.

The next ball was similar, maybe a fraction fuller. Stokes, unwilling to leave it after what had just happened, tried to sweep it from outside off. He got an under-edge, and Hadds took a great catch. As so often in this series, Nathan Lyon had got the vital breakthrough.

From there, things progressed quickly. Graeme Swann slogged Nathan to the boundary, but then inside-edged one onto his pad and was caught close in. Stuart Broad came out, looking very tender on his bruised foot. The Barmy Army were singing with great gusto, as they often do when they are staring defeat in the face, and we responded by motioning to the rest of the crowd to make a bit of noise. They obliged.

It was getting really exciting now. There was still some great cricket to come. In the over after Swann's dismissal, Mitch bowled a slower ball to Bresnan, who made clean contact but got through his drive a bit early. The ball flew to deepish mid-off, between where Chris Rogers was fielding and the bowler. Chris ran around on his nearly 37-year-old legs and leapt horizontally . . . to catch the ball brilliantly before hitting the turf. We were all running around high-fiving and embracing, it was such a great way to get the last of the dangerous batsmen out.

We kept throwing everything into every ball. Just like in Brisbane, when the last batsman came to the wicket, we were as intense and unrelenting as if it was the first ball of the innings. James Anderson joined Broad. Mitch, with the second ball of his 26th over, the 104th of the innings, put a short one into Anderson's ribs. Anderson fended it away, only to pop it up to short leg. It hung in the air and then fell into George Bailey's cupped hands. After the way Anderson confronted George in Brisbane, the manner of this last dismissal, to seal the Ashes, had a bit of karma about it.

What happened next is a bit of a blur. Brad Haddin ran over to me and picked me up, shouting that the Ashes were coming back home. We then raced up to the rest of the boys and embraced mid-pitch. We were shouting and screaming and carrying on. We broke the huddle to shake hands with Anderson and Broad, and continued celebrating before breaking again to go through the post-match formalities. For me, that meant a presentation on the field and a press conference before I could join the boys in the changing room and start the party in earnest.

There was a bit of relief in there that we hadn't let England get too close or make today too much of a nervous ordeal. Before lunch, there were signs that this was going to be a long and tense day. But after lunch, we finished the Test match off quick and clean. I was also relieved that we had converted our outstanding play in the past three weeks into three wins. It would have been such a shame not to get full value for our dominance.

Overwhelming those feelings of relief, coming over everything like a big wave, was our excitement about winning the Ashes. I am ecstatic that we have done it so convincingly and will go to the Melbourne and Sydney Test matches having already won. Everyone wants to know how we have done it, how we have turned 0–3 into 3–0 in such a short space of time. If you boil it down, as a team, we just got sick of losing. A lot of the excitement can be put down to that. We remember the pain all too well, and after such pain, the pleasure is twice as great.

We invited wives and children to the changing room for an hour. Having been brought up in the traditional style, where families were not part of the changing room environment, I am all in favour of keeping the room as an inner sanctum for the team and support staff, but today it was appropriate to relax the boundaries and welcome our loved ones in. They have given us so much, it was important to let them share it with us. They are a part of the success the players and support staff have had. Some parents and family members came in too, which was lovely.

Once they left, it was just the team for a few hours, talking and celebrating in each other's company. Darren Lehmann did his customary debrief. He said a few simple words about what a great reward this was for our hard work, and the emotion in the room was high. Then our manager, Gavin Dovey, came forward and presented me with a gift from the team for my hundredth Test match: a framed picture of me walking onto the WACA during this match, with scoresheets of both this match and my Test debut in Bangalore back in 2004. Along with it came a bottle of Penfolds Grange Hermitage 2004 vintage, to mark the date of my first Test match, and a certificate for a bottle of the 2013 vintage, which will be released in 2017. I am so grateful for the gift, and for the greater gift that these people have given me on and off the field.

I spoke a few words to the group, thanking them, and saying how 2004 feels just like yesterday. It has gone so quickly. I urged them to enjoy and cherish the good times like today. This is the pinnacle!

There are so many special parts of a day I want to remember forever. As soon as the game finished,

Shane Watson came over to me with a stump. He had salvaged it and wanted me to have it. This has been a great game for Watto, and finding a stump to give me was a nice gesture after the 15 years of cricket we have played together.

Nathan Lyon led us in the team song on the middle of the WACA Ground, and then we staged a re-enactment of Chris Rogers's catch of Tim Bresnan at mid-off, not with a ball this time, but with a stubby of beer. He dived and caught it again.

Tonight, we capped the celebration by heading to the Crown Metropol at Burswood, where Shane Warne threw the team a party. His villa was like a house, the best hotel suite you have ever seen. There can't be many people on earth who love seeing the Australian team do well as much as Warnie does. He certainly knows how to throw a party, and generously ensured that the wives and partners were included as well as the team. We stayed there until late, and then came back to the hotel. It has been a great night, and I want to give big thanks to Crown and Shane for putting on a fantastic function where we could let our hair down in private.

I can't keep the smile off my face.

Wednesday 18 December. Perth to Sydney.

We flew to our home towns today, some of us nursing bigger hangovers than others. Those of us on the Sydney flight had a bit of a testing time, putting up with a delay of about two or three hours, but nothing can dampen our spirits. I am very tired, but on a high. Over the next couple of days, I am really looking forward to getting around and saying thank you to friends and others who have helped me get here – not only to play 100 Test matches, but to have helped get my body into shape to make a contribution in this series. I owe them everything. Winning this Ashes series has been my total priority, and to have achieved it is something I can give back to those who have supported me.

I have been reflecting a lot on where we were at earlier this year and how quickly things have changed. In April, we were described as the worst Australian team ever to have toured India. Now, this series is being described as one of the best Ashes wins ever. That is a lesson for us all. If you keep faith in your own ability and do your work, everything can turn in your favour, and fast. Never give up, and never stop believing. Those words can sound like empty slogans, but the Australian Test cricket team has just lived them. It happens. I am sure that if we hadn't lost those series in India and England and felt so disrespected, we would not be enjoying our comeback quite as much.

In England, when things were at their lowest, I often referred in my diary to the times I looked at the photograph on my iPad of the waves crashing into the near shore and the calmness out on the horizon.

As I wrote in my diary of that tour, I often had to blot out the turmoil of the moment and think of the distant horizon that represented our future, when we would achieve what we were aiming for. Sometimes it seemed very distant! When I got back to Australia from England, I broke my iPad and changed to an iPad Mini. One of the first things I did was transfer that photograph onto the new device so I could keep looking at it.

Our horizon is not just winning the Ashes. It's getting back to number one in the world. That job is far from done. Today we are one step closer.

Third Test

13–17 December 2013. Western Australia Cricket Association Ground, Perth.

Australia (first innings)

Batting		R	B	4	6	SR
CJL Rogers	run out (Anderson)	11	9	2	0	122.22
DA Warner	c: Carberry b: Swann	60	77	8	1	77.92
SR Watson	c: Swann b: Broad	18	29	3	0	62.06
MJ Clarke	c: Cook b: Swann	24	44	5	0	54.54
SPD Smith	c: Prior b: Anderson	111	208	14	2	53.36
GJ Bailey	c: Pietersen b: Broad	7	12	1	0	58.33
BJ Haddin	c: Anderson b: Stokes	55	100	5	2	55.00
MG Johnson	c: Prior b: Broad	39	62	6	0	62.90
PM Siddle	c: Prior b: Bresnan	21	36	3	0	58.33
RJ Harris	c: Root b: Anderson	12	19	1	0	63.15
NM Lyon	not out	17	25	4	0	68.00
Extras	(6lb, 3w, 1nb, 0b)	10				
Total	10 Wkts, 103.3 overs	385		3.71 Runs/Over		

Fall of wickets 1-85 (Carberry, 25.4 ov), 2-90 (Root, 30.5 ov), 3-136 (Cook, 48.4 ov), 4-146 (Pietersen, 51.5 ov), 5-190 (Bell, 70.3 ov), 6-198 (Stokes, 73.6 ov), 7-207 (Prior, 77.3 ov), 8-229 (Broad, 81.4 ov), 9-233 (Bresnan, 84.1 ov),10-251 (Anderson, 87.6 ov)

Bowling	O	M	R	W	Econ	SR	Extras
JM Anderson	23	5	60	2	2.60	69	(1w)
SCJ Broad	22	2	100	3	4.54	44	(1w)
TT Bresnan	23.3	4	81	1	3.44	141	
BA Stokes	17	3	63	1	3.70	102	(1nb, 1w)
GP Swann	17	0	71	2	4.17	54	
JE Root	1	0	4	0	4.00	–	

England (first innings)

Batting		R	B	4	6	SR
AN Cook	c: Warner b: Lyon	72	153	10	0	47.05
MA Carberry	b: Harris	43	76	8	1	56.57
JE Root	c: Haddin b: Watson	4	16	1	0	25.00
KP Pietersen	c: Johnson b: Siddle	19	59	3	0	32.20
IR Bell	lbw: Harris	15	71	2	0	21.12
BA Stokes	c: Haddin b: Johnson	18	57	3	0	31.57
MJ Prior	c: Haddin b: Siddle	8	24	1	0	33.33
TT Bresnan	c: Haddin b: Harris	21	29	4	0	72.41
SCJ Broad	lbw: Johnson	5	13	1	0	38.46
GP Swann	not out	19	23	4	0	82.60
JM Anderson	c: Bailey b: Siddle	2	9	0	0	22.22
Extras	(7lb, 5w, 2nb, 11b)	25				
Total	10 Wkts, 88 overs	251		2.85 Runs/Over		

Fall of wickets 1-85 (Carberry, 25.4 ov), 2-90 (Root, 30.5 ov), 3-136 (Cook, 48.4 ov), 4-146 (Pietersen, 51.5 ov), 5-190 (Bell, 70.3 ov), 6-198 (Stokes, 73.6 ov), 7-207 (Prior, 77.3 ov), 8-229 (Broad, 81.4 ov), 9-233 (Bresnan, 84.1 ov),10-251 (Anderson, 87.6 ov)

Bowling	O	M	R	W	Econ	SR	Extras
RJ Harris	22	10	48	3	2.18	44	(1nb)
MG Johnson	22	7	62	2	2.81	66	(1nb)
SR Watson	12	3	48	1	4.00	72	
PM Siddle	16	5	36	3	2.25	32	(5w)
NM Lyon	16	6	39	1	2.43	96	

Australia (second innings)

Batting		R	B	4	6	SR
CJL Rogers	c: Carberry b: Bresnan	54	135	8	0	40.00
DA Warner	c: Stokes b: Swann	112	140	17	2	80.00
SR Watson	run out (Bresnan)	103	108	11	5	95.37
MJ Clarke	b: Stokes	23	53	2	0	43.39
SPD Smith	c: sub (JM Bairstow) b: Stokes	15	50	0	0	30.00
GJ Bailey	not out	39	30	3	3	130.00
BJ Haddin	c: Swann b: Bresnan	5	6	1	0	83.33
MG Johnson	not out	0	0	0	0	-
PM Siddle						
RJ Harris						
NM Lyon						
Extras	(5lb, 5w, 0nb, 8b)	18				
Total	6 Wkts, 87 overs	369		4.24 Runs/Over		

Fall of wickets 1-157 (Rogers, 43.1 ov), 2-183 (Warner, 48.5 ov), 3-223 (Clarke, 63.5 ov), 4-301 (Smith, 79.1 ov), 5-331 (Watson, 83.1 ov), 6-340 (Haddin, 85.4 ov)

Bowling	O	M	R	W	Econ	SR	Extras
JM Anderson	19	5	105	0	5.52	-	(1w)
TT Bresnan	14	3	53	2	3.78	42	
BA Stokes	18	1	82	2	4.55	54	
GP Swann	27	8	92	1	3.40	162	
JE Root	9	1	24	0	2.66	-	

England (second innings)

Batting		R	B	4	6	SR
AN Cook	b: Harris	0	1	0	0	0.00
MA Carberry	lbw: Watson	31	53	6	0	58.49
JE Root	c: Haddin b: Johnson	19	88	1	0	21.59
KP Pietersen	c: Harris b: Lyon	45	57	6	1	78.94
IR Bell	c: Haddin b: Siddle	60	93	7	1	64.51
BA Stokes	c: Haddin b: Lyon	120	195	18	1	61.53
MJ Prior	c: Haddin b: Johnson	26	72	3	0	36.11
TT Bresnan	c: Rogers b: Johnson	12	40	1	0	30.00
GP Swann	c: Smith b: Lyon	4	6	1	0	66.66
SCJ Broad	not out	2	7	0	0	28.57
JM Anderson	c: Bailey b: Johnson	2	8	0	0	25.00
Extras	(13lb, 6w, 0nb, 13b)	32				
Total	10 Wkts, 103.2 overs	353		3.41 Runs/Over		

Fall of wickets 1-0 (Cook, 0.1 ov), 2-62 (Carberry, 18.6 ov), 3-76 (Root, 27.3 ov), 4-121 (Pietersen, 39.2 ov), 5-220 (Bell, 59.6 ov), 6-296 (Prior, 85.2 ov), 7-336 (Stokes, 98.2 ov), 8-347 (Swann, 100.2 ov), 9-349 (Bresnan, 101.3 ov), 10-353 (Anderson, 103.2 ov)

Bowling	O	M	R	W	Econ	SR	Extras
RJ Harris	19	2	73	1	3.84	114	
MG Johnson	25.2	6	78	4	3.07	38	(5w)
NM Lyon	22	5	70	3	3.18	34	(1w)
PM Siddle	26	11	67	1	2.57	156	
SR Watson	11	1	39	1	3.54	66	

5

THE FOURTH TEST MATCH

Thursday 19 December. Sydney.

My body has been pretty tired since we flew back in to Sydney and my emotions have felt drained out of me, which is possibly not surprising after two back-to-back Test matches, the second one played in extreme heat. So this morning, to start freshening myself up, I did some cardio training and then went to Beecroft to see my physio Steve and spend a session on the MedX machine. My back is not in bad shape, but like I always say, time spent on that contraption is money in the bank.

From there, I went to ANZ Stadium at Homebush, the base for my Big Bash League team, the Sydney Thunder. The team didn't win a game last summer, and during the off-season the whole management, coaching and leadership set-up has been revamped. Chandika Hathurusinghe, the former Sri Lankan international player who is one of the coaches at Cricket NSW, has come in as coach of the Thunder, and Mike Hussey has been brought over from the Perth Scorchers. Although Mike has retired from Test cricket, he was the leading run-scorer in the last Indian Premier League season, and in the opinion of many good judges is still one of the most valuable Twenty20 batsmen in the world. It will be good being part of the squad with Mike, after so many years in the Australian team together. But I won't be on the field, as my contract with the franchise is in a marketing rather than playing capacity. Nominally, I am the captain, but I expect to be fully committed to playing for the Australian Test and one-day teams during the BBL season.

We had a signing session, a team photo, and media interviews at ANZ, after which I watched the boys preparing for their first match, which is against the Sydney Sixers at the Sydney Cricket Ground on Saturday night. It was good to see a few of the sponsors, whom I know already, and the players.

Back at home tonight, I am planning to catch up with some of the people who have helped me on my journey to this point. Even though our Ashes-winning Test match is a couple of days ago, the glow is still very much present and I would like to get around and say thanks.

Friday 20 December. **Sydney.**

As we will be down in Melbourne for Christmas, Kyly and I invited our families over to our place tonight for our Christmas do. It has become our tradition to hold the big family get-together the weekend before Christmas. We have had plenty of food and a couple of glasses of wine, and it was a great way to reflect on the year and enjoy each other's company.

There were a couple of other reasons to celebrate. It was my grandfather's 80th birthday, and the 45th wedding anniversary for Kyly's parents. So it was a special occasion for both sides of the family. My sister and sister-in-law both have young sons, so we had a lot of fun giving them presents and spoiling them rotten. Kyly and I don't get too much time with our families, so that makes nights like tonight all the more special.

Saturday 21 December. **Sydney.**

First thing this morning, I intensified my training, focusing on cardio and strength work. My plan is to up my cardio work in the gym so I will be fresh and fit for the Boxing Day Test match, to do some strength work with Duncan Kerr, and to get more work done on my back. It is hard to get these sessions done while on tour, when you are concentrating on your cricket skills, so when I get some days at home I go back to these fitness fundamentals.

Yesterday I did three separate sessions, and today I did two sessions, each lasting just over an hour. My purpose is, as much as anything, to get my mind where I want it to be for the Melbourne Test match: just straightening it all out and getting back into my personal zone after all the excitement and emotional peak of winning the Ashes in Perth.

Tonight is the first Thunder game of BBL03. I will be watching at the SCG and supporting my team against the Sixers, who have included Steve Smith, one of the three Australian Test players who have been released for this BBL round. Everyone at the Thunder is hoping for a much improved season.

Sunday 22 December. Melbourne.

I flew down to Melbourne this morning. As I got off the plane, I heard some stunning news: Graeme Swann had announced his retirement. I am extremely shocked. I certainly did not expect that.

I don't know what to say. I will be among the first to pay my respects and compliments towards Swanny as a man and as a cricketer. He has been a fantastic player for a long time for England, and has achieved a hell of a lot. His statistics speak for themselves. He has taken 255 wickets in 60 Tests, which places him in the top handful of all-time England wicket-takers, and he has also played a lot of one-day internationals. England will definitely miss him for his bowling, his slips catching and his good-humoured mood around the group. From a distance, he comes across as one of the guys who, when you are on tour, you would want to have around, because he usually manages to find the light side to everything. He is a big loss to England and it is a major surprise, coming three Test matches into the series. I haven't heard any more details yet about his reasons for retiring at this moment. All I can say is that I am shocked.

Personally, I have had some great challenges against Swanny. Our batting plans in England this year revolved in large part around countering him on those dry wickets. He spun the ball a lot for a finger-spinner, had great control, and got left-handers out for fun. As a right-hander, I found him difficult because of his natural variation, change of pace and spin. He was always a thinking bowler, and the mental challenge of facing him was unrelenting. As an opponent, I can't praise him highly enough.

From the airport we drove into Melbourne, where our boys were gathering at the team hotel. When I got there, everyone was talking about Swanny. In his press conference, he said he was retiring because he had simply had enough, and couldn't contribute positively to the touring group anymore. As they say, when a voice in a player's head says it is time to finish, then it is time to finish. Swanny said that he weighed up the pros and cons of battling his way through the rest of the tour, and had come to the decision that by hanging on while not feeling enthusiastic about his cricket he would be doing more harm than good. There has been a bit of negative comment about him pulling out during a tour, rather than waiting until the end, but I don't know enough about the situation to comment on it. I suppose I am just glad I won't have him trying to get me out anymore.

Once we had settled in, we did our usual routine of rehab, recovery and screening before getting together with Cricket Australia staff for a Christmas party at the hotel. It was mainly a matter of conveying our appreciation to the back-room staff, who don't get to come on tour, for their support through the year. Winning the Ashes certainly puts some sparkle into gatherings like these. There were plenty of family members there, with kids running around, which adds some excitement to Christmas. There is some rain around in Melbourne, but we are all excited about getting onto the Melbourne Cricket Ground for training tomorrow and preparing for this great occasion.

Monday 23 December. Melbourne.

We had a great practice session today. I was watching the boys closely for any signs that they might be letting up on their intensity after Perth. The last thing we want to think, or even feel subconsciously, is that we can take it easy after winning the Ashes. From our point of view, the job is not done. We are playing ten Test matches against England this year and so far the score is 3–3. On top of that, we are playing a Test match for our country. No other motivation is necessary. And I am very pleased to report that the boys have trained as enthusiastically and professionally today as they have all summer.

There is some injury-related anxiety over Shane Watson, who strained his calf while doing some private training in Sydney after returning from Perth. He only bowled one over in the nets today before pulling up. The plan is to take him slow and steady. His ability to bowl, or not bowl, could influence the selectors in how they choose the Test eleven, but we are not sure yet and won't be until we see how Shane's recovery progresses.

I took a look at the MCG's drop-in wicket while we were at the ground. It has a fair bit of grass on it, so I will be scrutinising it tomorrow and on Christmas Day to see if that changes. It might make for interesting decisions at the toss in three days' time.

Tuesday 24 December. **Melbourne.**

Another training session this morning, and things for the most part went well. Everyone trained hard, and I am pleased with the boys. There's no post-Ashes winning let-down that I can see.

Shane Watson's calf is still hurting him but it's getting better slowly, and he bowled three overs today. We also have some concerns about our stiff and sore fast bowlers. Ryan Harris's knee is inflamed, while Peter Siddle and Mitchell Johnson are both aching still after that long slog through the Adelaide and Perth Test matches. We will have to watch them all closely.

At our team meeting, we talked about Graeme Swann being out of the England team and who will replace him. Monty Panesar is obviously the logical pick. There might be other changes too. England have a few new players in their squad whom we haven't seen much of, and in Perth obviously Ben Stokes got the jump on us. With the Ashes lost, they might be tempted to bring in some fresh blood, so we have had a bit of a chat about the possible replacements and how we plan to counter them. But we won't know anything for sure until England name their team. As for us, it would be nice to keep the same eleven together for a fourth Test match, but we have to be sensible about risking the bowlers and their injuries.

Wednesday 25 December.
Melbourne. Christmas Day.

Christmas is always special with the Australian cricket team. You never know how many Christmas Days you will have like this, so my attitude is to make the most of every one.

We had another good training session this morning, with all the usual routines, getting our gear ready in the changing rooms and setting ourselves up individually for match day.

After practice, the team and their partners and children went to Crown for Christmas lunch. Peter Siddle and Chris Rogers, who are based here in Melbourne, weren't there, as they were given permission to spend Christmas lunch with their families. The rest of us had a fun few hours, with Kris Kringle presents handed out among the team members, staff and loved ones.

Kyly and I went from there to Shane Warne's house, where we had a swim, lounged around the pool and spent a normal kind of Christmas Day. Warnie had his family over – his kids, his parents, his brother Jason and Jason's family. For Kyly and me, because we can't be with our own families, Warnie's place feels like a home away from home. I like to get over there every Christmas Day.

Then it was back to the hotel and getting ready for the Test match. It's funny: we have won the Ashes, but I am still as nervous as ever.

Thursday 26 December. Melbourne.

It has been another interesting day, to say the least, and I am still stirred up about a few things that affected us before the Test match started.

Shane Watson's calf strain had restricted him to bowling just four overs in the nets in the three days since we have been in Melbourne. I know him and his history very well, and can clearly remember what happened last Boxing Day Test match, when a similar calf strain brought him down and kept him out of the Sydney Test match. It continued to bother him through the first part of the year, and it disrupted our plans during the tour of India.

Watto's bowling is a vital element in the balance of our team. If he can't bowl the overs we need, there is the potential of a knock-on effect that really worries me. Considering the loads that Ryan Harris, Mitchell Johnson and Peter Siddle have carried in the first three Test matches, the contribution Watto makes is essential in keeping those three guys on the field. If they hadn't had the respite Watto gives them, there would have been every chance that at least one of them might have picked up a serious injury. On top of that, my strategy to bowl Mitch in short, incisive spells relies at times on those overs we get out of Watto. All the parts fit together. The fifth bowler is crucial.

So I have been increasingly concerned since Watto picked up this calf strain. I talked to the selectors, and to Darren Lehmann, who is of course a selector himself, and they were confident that Watto could get through the game as an all-rounder.

When England were just two wickets down today, Watto pulled up during his run-up. The calf was tender, but he had also now tweaked his groin. I am really concerned that the longer England bat in this match, the more chance the three main bowlers are of getting injured. That has cost us Test matches in the past, notably in Adelaide last year, when losing James Pattinson definitely cost us a win in that match against South Africa. I do not want to see it happen again.

The other issue giving me a restless night is that after winning the toss this morning I put England in to bat. I have done this before in Test matches, but it's a rare thing if you look through history. There used to be the saying that you always bat first, except on the occasions when you think about it for a while and *then* bat first. While I was growing up and watching the Australian team, Mark Taylor and Steve Waugh wanted to bat first almost without exception. It was the orthodox thing to do, and they had the benefit of great bowlers such as Shane Warne and Glenn McGrath to bowl teams out in the fourth innings. But in my career, it has become less uncommon to put opponents in, and I have done it a few times. I try to sum up the situation and physical conditions, both on the wicket and, just as importantly, overhead. I think of the make-up of our bowling attack, and ask myself how they would use the conditions. The underlying principle is always attack: whether it's batting first or bowling first, I try to choose whichever option will give us the initiative in the game.

Today, when I first looked at the wicket I thought it was one of those pitches when you consider bowling, but then decide to bat. I didn't have my spikes on, so I didn't have the ability to feel what the turf was like underneath the surface. I looked at the overhead conditions, which were cloudy, quite solidly overcast, with some rain around the central Melbourne area.

When a decision hangs in the balance like this, I look to the experienced heads around me. I spoke to Darren Lehmann and Brad Haddin. I sought the counsel of Mark Taylor and Shane Warne, whose cricket brains and instincts I respect so much. Everyone had diverse ideas and suggestions. There was no clear consensus on whether we should bat or bowl if we won the toss.

Before walking out to the toss with Alastair Cook, I told the team that if I won the call, we would be batting. But I was still unsure. I can't remember ever being so uncertain at the moment of the toss. But I had spikes on now, and when we walked onto the pitch the feeling I got through my feet was that the spikes were penetrating and the wicket was tackier, a little more damp, than I had expected. Some more rain had swept through Melbourne in the meantime. I guess I just asked my gut.

I would have been happy to lose the toss for once, and leave the deciding to Cookie. But I was 'lucky' again, and won. My gut feeling, at that instant, was to ask England to bat. I know a lot of people will be asking questions about my decision, and will be ready to criticise it, based on the outcomes in the first session, the first day, the first innings, and the course of the match. In my view, all of those intermediate milestones are important, but it is the result of the Test match that stands as the final judgement.

So the team, no doubt to the surprise of some, found out we had won the toss and were bowling. We were excited when we lined up for the national anthems. There was a massive crowd in, and by the end of the day it passed the world record for a game of cricket, around 91,000. It shows how solidly Australians have got behind our team this summer, as well as the large numbers of travelling fans from England and elsewhere. Funnily enough, George Bailey had been expecting to be among the crowd. A couple of months ago, he bought tickets for himself and his dad to come up from Tasmania as spectators. And here he is, getting a much closer view!

We were generally a bit off our game all day, compared with the standards we maintained in Brisbane, Adelaide and Perth. The new-ball attack was looser than usual, and in the field we were misfielding balls that up to now we have been capturing cleanly. Cook got off to a good start, scoring his first 20 at a run a ball. The ball was not seaming as much as I had expected, and very early in the session I began to worry about whether I had made a critical mistake by electing to bowl first. I took Mitch off after two overs. Ryan, meanwhile, was producing a few half-chances but we weren't good enough in the field to back him up. Michael Carberry edged him to my left at second slip, but Smithy was ultra-keen beside me and dived across in front, putting the catch down. Rhino also had Cook edging a couple of times, and playing and missing, but we didn't get that spark that might have given us the feeling that we hold the momentum in the game.

I brought Peter Siddle on for Mitch from the Members end, to tighten things up. If we weren't taking wickets with Plan A, we had to look at alternative ways of getting them. Sidds bowled a good long spell, cutting Cook's scoring down to seven runs in about 45 minutes. Unwilling to risk Watto so early, I also brought Nathan Lyon on from the Southern Stand end in the ninth over to replace Rhino. It mustn't have looked very good, bringing a spinner on during the first hour on a day when I have put the opposition in to bat. But as Warnie keeps telling me, 'When it seams, it spins.' It can be good to get a spinner on early. In addition, both of the batsmen were left-handers, and Lyono could turn the ball away from them. He bowled a really tight four-over spell, only conceding five runs.

Sidds has been fantastic this year, without maybe grabbing the headlines like Mitch and Rhino. He has often got us vital wickets, and so it was again this morning when he frustrated Cook for a long time before angling one across him, just on a back-foot length, that Cook reached for and nicked to me at second slip. When they reflect on this Ashes campaign, people should not forget Sidds's knack for bowling excellent dry spells that have resulted consistently in pressure and wickets.

This was a perfect demonstration of why he is so crucial to our bowling plans.

With the first wicket down, I brought Mitch back on, from the Southern Stand end this time, and he was much better, getting his speed up into the high 140s and hitting the new batsman, Joe Root, with a bouncer on the shoulder. Rhino came back from the Members end, and was immediately close to trapping Root LBW.

With Root and Carberry surviving, I rolled the dice and gave Watto a couple of overs before the break. He seemed okay at first. A full out-swinger just curved past Root's off stump in Watto's first over, and in the next over, as some light drizzle blew in, Rhino thought he had Carberry LBW when he padded up. We referred the not-out decision to DRS, and the ball-tracker suggested it might have clipped the off bail, but it was not definitive enough to overturn the on-field umpire's opinion. So England went into lunch at 1/71, what they would consider a pretty solid start after being sent in to bat and a result we felt was not quite good enough for us. Our bowlers had created enough chances, though, so we said before going back out that if we kept plugging away we ought to be able to turn it around.

Rhino had only given up five runs in eight overs in the first session, so I started the afternoon with him and Watto. But Rhino started with a bad ball down the leg-side and then over-pitched for Root to drive him away through the off, so I gave him a rest and attacked with Mitch while containing with Watto.

We have had good plans for Carberry, feeding his favoured cut shot and then cramping him from around the wicket. So it played out today. He got a nice cut away off Watto, who then switched the angle. Two balls later, Watto bowled a beautiful curling in-swinger from around the wicket. Carberry didn't offer a shot. The ball kept coming in, and took out his off stump. I am a lucky captain to be able to depend on Sidds and Watto if the new-ball guys haven't broken through. Watto's bowling, in my opinion, is generally underrated. He takes a lot of wickets for the bowler at the other end, by frustrating batsmen or keeping them on or off strike, or many other ways that don't necessarily go down in the scorebook.

With Kevin Pietersen coming in, I brought Sidds back to replace Watto, whom I did not want to over-tax. Pietersen was his usual self, anxious to get off his duck and uncertain against Sidds. Meanwhile Mitch was firing up against Root, getting his speed up past 150 kilometres per hour. There were great personal duels going on at both ends. By the drinks break, Root and Pietersen had managed to stay at the wicket, but we felt that we weren't far away from breaking through.

I kept Sidds on after drinks, but brought Rhino back from the Members end. He wasn't happy with his two overs after lunch, but he has great resilience and usually manages to think his way through any temporary issue. His first ball of his new spell was perfect, on off stump and nipping away. Root had to play at it and feathered the edge to Brad Haddin. What a comeback from a great bowler.

What followed was a very slow, tight period. Pietersen and Bell must have resolved to wear our bowlers down with defence. It became a battle of patience. I replaced Sidds with Watto, and he bowled his usual mean line and length. But two overs into this new spell, he grimaced after bowling a ball to Pietersen. He ran in and bowled another, and my worst fears were realised when he said he had injured his groin. I am extremely concerned about the effect this might have on the workload of our seam bowlers.

It's all relative, and we have got used to many one-percenters going our way in the first three Test matches. But the rub of the green was with England today. This is cricket, and you have to ride these ups and downs whether they're going for you or the opponent. There were the edges that fell short, the chances put down, the close LBW appeals, and now Watto's breakdown. Three overs after Watto went off, Pietersen had another life. He had spent a long time scoring six singles, and then Rhino dropped short and Pietersen tried to hook it. He top-edged, and we thought the ball was going straight to Nathan Coulter-Nile, who was substituting for Watto and fielding at deep fine leg. Nathan caught the ball, but his momentum was taking him back towards the boundary rope. Thinking he was going to fall over, he tossed the ball in the air, intending to catch it inside the field of play. It is a type of catch that used to be rare but has become increasingly common since the advent of Twenty20 cricket, when batsmen are trying to hit so many sixes. Nathan looked like he had executed it all right, but with the movement of his body the ball lobbed up and over the rope with him. The chance had gone, and Pietersen's six had doubled his score.

Through the afternoon and into the evening session, we worked away at Pietersen and Bell. I shifted the fields around and tried a few plans, but the Englishmen were not taking any risks, aside from one time when Pietersen tried a quick single to get off strike to Nathan Lyon, and George Bailey just missed with his throw. It was pretty slow cricket.

On the last ball before the final-session drinks break, we finally broke the partnership. Ryan Harris is so relentlessly accurate, and he was able to get a little bit of reverse swing as the ball grew old. The pitch is really roughing it up, and there should be some reverse for all the seamers. After more than two hours, Bell nicked one, and we had ended what we felt was the key partnership.

Even though the wickets were not coming in a rush, the runs weren't either. That was the saving grace of the day. We had already put down Carberry and Pietersen, and then dropped Pietersen again when he toe-ended a pull off Rhino to mid-wicket and George Bailey put down the chance. Afterwards, the game was held up for quite a while as Kevin began vomiting to the side of the wicket.

Apparently he has been quite unwell, and he was certainly struggling out there.

The second new ball changed the tone of the day. Everything had been grinding along for hours, and then Mitch bowled a really fast spell from the Members end. He had Ben Stokes nicking the third delivery to first slip. After Stokes's fine innings in Perth, we knew what a critical wicket that was. A couple of overs later, Jonny Bairstow, whom England had brought in to replace Matt Prior as wicketkeeper, tried to take Mitch on, skying an attempted hook over slips for six and then cutting him forward of point. Next ball, Mitch ripped through Bairstow with sheer pace, and we had six down. As things heated up in that late spell, Mitch and Rhino could have had a couple more wickets, so we are looking forward to getting stuck in with that new ball tomorrow morning.

All up, I am feeling a little uneasy, as I have all day. Watto's injury worries me. If you ask the team, they will say it was a pretty good day for us to have England 6/226. We bowled too short with the new ball, but because England batted so slowly we can regard the day as fairly successful. Bowling first, I would have been content to have England out for 250 today. We don't have them all out, but we might have done so if we hadn't dropped three catches, and we may still have them out for 250 if we bowl and field well tomorrow morning.

My feeling right now, though, is uncertainty. I keep wondering if I should have chosen to bat first. Did I make a mistake? I'm wondering at this moment if I did, but the beauty of Test cricket is that we won't know until after the match has been decided.

Friday 27 December. Melbourne.

Our aim this morning was to get England for less than 300, and then bat well. I guess the first part of that plan worked out . . .

It was a cooler day, with the breeze blowing from the south and another large crowd in. Ryan Harris got things going from the Members end and Kevin Pietersen showed immediately that he was going to take a different approach from yesterday, slashing the first ball of the day over point for a boundary.

Things got busier in a hurry. Mitch Johnson was coming down-breeze, and his first ball was a snorter to Tim Bresnan, who could only parry it out of his ribs for George Bailey to take a well-judged catch running from bat-pad towards short backward square leg. As he showed yesterday with the second new ball, Mitch was going to be a real handful now. He bowled brilliantly, with pace and aggression. Pietersen tried to step away and smack him somewhere, anywhere, but missed once and then tried it again, two balls later, this time losing his leg stump. He had batted for so long yesterday in such a gritty, determined manner, but today he was gone in a flash.

Stuart Broad tried to counter-attack for a couple of overs, but when he went onto the back foot Mitch gave him the same in-swinging yorker with which he hurt Broad's foot in Perth, and the LBW was one of the easier decisions umpire Aleem Dar has had to make.

That meant five wickets in the innings for Mitch once again. He raised the ball in what has become the traditional gesture, but gave a special acknowledgement to the Barmy Army, who had been back to their old tricks yesterday, singing some fairly disrespectful lyrics to Mitch. His bowling was the best possible answer, and a few of us backed him up by turning to that section of the crowd and holding our fingers to our lips.

Nathan Lyon came on to take the last wicket, bowling Monty Panesar who didn't offer a stroke, and the morning could not have gone better. England were all out for 255. Last night I would have accepted 300, so this quick morning collapse was a bonus for us.

Still, we knew that the drop-in pitch was behaving with variable pace and bounce and offering ample movement off the seam. It's a rough-looking surface, too, which meant Broad and James Anderson might be able to extract some reverse swing. Our aim was to play positively, but to be watchful and select our shots well. In this, we failed.

David Warner and Chris Rogers started nicely, each driving fours down the ground. It looked like a pitch where you had to play straight, and wait for the one to hit.

Davey was trying to play his shots, but the uneven pace and bounce did him in when he top-edged an attempted pull off Anderson. Soon after, Shane Watson was out inside-edging a ball from Stokes that decked in and kept a little low, a sure sign that we were playing on a very different kind of wicket from what we saw in Perth.

Ben Stokes greeted me with two bouncers, but Chris and I got through to lunch unscathed. The game was looking more challenging now that England's bowlers were doing well with the new ball. Stokes and Broad bowled tightly to us after the break, and we played and missed a few times while struggling to come to terms with the conditions.

Very soon, there was a halt to play after Chris was hit on the head. Broad, who was bowling up in the high 140s now, sent down a good bouncer which Chris ducked, but it didn't get up and smashed into the right side of his protective grille. He crumpled to the ground. I rushed down the pitch, as did Broad and some of the English players, to see if he was all right. I was concerned about his safety, of course. He said he wasn't dizzy, and when Doc Peter Brukner and Alex Kountouris came out and spoke to him, he said he didn't have a headache and was seeing clearly. He could bat on, but the side of his helmet had hit his face so hard with the impact that it had opened a cut on the side of his face, and blood was running down his cheek. It was only a superficial wound though, and he was fine to keep going. After the interruption, he responded in the best possible way, with some cracking drives through the off-side and down the ground. His biggest issue was finding a replacement helmet that would fit his head. He kept calling for new ones until he was happier.

Bresnan and Anderson came on to replace Broad and Stokes, and they were also making the best of conditions that were very much in the bowlers' favour. I battled on for an hour, but just before the mid-session drinks break I made a poor misjudgement of a ball from Anderson that was coming in from the off-side. I left it, and it took the top of my off stump.

I am extremely disappointed with myself for leaving a ball and getting bowled. Two things I have worked on leading into this series were my back-foot play against the short ball, and also moving my guard a little towards the off-side to protect myself against being bowled. I might need to move across a little bit further still, so my toes are on middle stump rather than middle and leg. Twenty-two per cent of my Test dismissals have been bowled, and I hate that stat. By moving my guard across, I accept that I might get out LBW a little bit more, but I would prefer that to getting bowled. And nothing feels worse than being bowled without offering a stroke. It wasn't a bad ball, but I should not have let it go.

The way I look at it tonight, now that I have cooled down a little, is that it's one of the great things about this game that even after 101 Test matches you can learn from every dismissal and every mistake. I still feel my game can improve, and my back-foot play this summer has shown that. Halving my percentage of dismissals getting bowled, which is my aim, will lead to bigger and better results.

After I was out, Chris Rogers and Steve Smith went about their work with great concentration and care, and made it to the tea break together. We needed a big partnership to take us up past England's total. At tea, we were still 159 runs behind. To concede a first-innings lead on this wicket really worries me. Half an hour after tea, however, Smithy went after a wide one from Broad and cut it quite hard to second slip. It flew fast to Ian Bell, who got his hands up to it just in time to take the catch. That one hurt us, but worse was to come two overs later when Bucky Rogers miscued when trying to drive Bresnan, and gave Pietersen a catch running around from mid-off. Bucky had fought so hard for nearly four hours, and my initial assessment was that, like most of us, his shot selection had let him down. In the dressing room I asked why he, in that situation, being the type of player he is, and with more than 60 runs on the board, would have risked lofting Bresnan down the ground. That was how it looked. But Chris assured me that he had tried to drive the ball along the turf straight of mid-off, but the ball had popped off the wicket, catching the bat fairly high on the face and causing him to hit it in the air. I was prepared to take his word for it. Still, I was so curious about how the pitch was behaving that I went to our video analyst Dene Hills and checked a side-on replay.

Sure enough, the ball had jumped alarmingly on Bucky. This pitch was really capable of playing up.

Brad Haddin went out there and, almost predictably, hit the ball cleaner and better than anyone from either side. He just has all the confidence in the world at the moment. You wish you could bottle some of that stuff and share it around. At the other end, George Bailey fought and fought and eventually sparred at a wideish one from Anderson. The English appealed, but the umpire gave him not out and George didn't think he had hit it. Alastair Cook referred it to DRS, which showed no Hot Spot mark on the bat. But the real-time Snickometer suggested there was a noise as the ball passed the bat, and the third umpire took this as enough evidence to overrule the on-field umpire. George still didn't think he had hit it, and it was a contentious decision in the circumstances.

Hadds kept going brilliantly, however, and we crossed our fingers hoping that he and Mitch could repeat what they did in Brisbane. Mitch was dropped at short cover, a fairly straightforward chance to Anderson, and we thought the rub of the green might be turning our way. Then Hadds, on 35, was given out LBW off Monty Panesar, but he referred it to the third umpire and the replay showed that the ball was missing the leg stump. The momentum felt like it really could be swinging back to us.

But an over after that referral, Mitch middled a pull shot off Bresnan straight to mid-wicket, where Anderson held the catch. Rhino and Sidds followed soon after, a big blow, and there are limits to what even Hadds can do for us tomorrow. We are 9/164, nearly 100 behind England, and our bowling successes of the morning seem a long time ago. It has been without a doubt our worst batting performance of the series so far. Both teams have found it hard to score freely on a two-paced wicket, but our shot selection was very poor. It has been a disappointing afternoon.

One of the worst things we can do in this situation is to look backwards. We have to look ahead and figure out a way to win the match. With that in mind, I have decided to stop dwelling on my decision at the toss yesterday and wondering if I did the right or wrong thing. Whatever happens, I am not going to second-guess or regret it. We bowled England out for 255, which is a good result after sending them in. The wicket is no worse for batting on today, so I am content that it was the right decision. While we are in this with a chance, I am not going to waste my energy on thinking about something that happened before the Test match started.

Saturday 28 December. Melbourne.

Today has been an amazing day in all respects. It has proved to me that our team has not allowed our standards to slip even though the Ashes are safe. The determination

Is there a better sight? A world record crowd of 91,092 watched us at the MCG on Boxing Day. Down on the field, though, I was wrestling with big decisions.

Some downtime with Kyly and our dog. I'm a lucky man.

My dad Les is the fiercest supporter of the Australian team I know. It was an emotional moment when he joined us in the changing room.

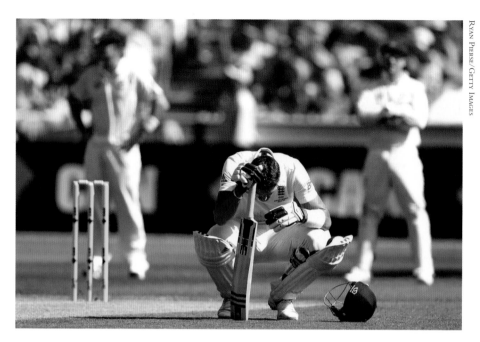

It was reported that he had swallowed a fly, but Kevin Pietersen was ill during his second innings in Melbourne. He battled on and was England's highest scorer in the series.

The Barmy Army was into Mitch on the first day in Melbourne. It was such a pleasure to see him bounce back with another man of the match performance. Offering him some moral support was the least we could do!

Rhino was struggling with knee and foot injuries as the Melbourne Test match ground on, but nothing could stop him. He was enjoying himself too much, and I was enjoying giving him the ball.

Michael Dodge / Getty Images

Michael Dodge / Getty Images

Chris Rogers was hit on the side of the face by Stuart Broad during the first innings. I was concerned about him at first, but his main problem was getting a replacement helmet to fit his head! He was our best batsman in the match, following a half-century in that first innings with a wonderful hundred in the second.

Gareth Copley / Getty Images

Michael Carberry and Alastair Cook about to bat in the second innings in Melbourne. Cook batted really well that day and threatened to take the match away from us.

Nathan Lyon had been thinking about tying down an end, but I told him his job was to take wickets. He duly delivered, with his career-best performance in Australia on a wicket that wasn't offering spin.

My favourite place to play cricket? The Sydney Cricket Ground. It's not a bad feeling, coming home to lead Australia with a 4-0 advantage in the series.

Spontaneously, without planning it, our team linked arms during the national anthem. Hadds and I provide a picture of the spirit of togetherness in the group.

Steve Smith evolved into a mainstay of the Australian team with three Ashes centuries in the space of six matches. In Sydney, he and Hadds rode their luck with some aggressive counter-attacking cricket.

MATT KING/GETTY IMAGES

There's only one Richie Benaud. Or is there? The Richies turned out in tribute on day two in Sydney.

RYAN PIERSE/GETTY IMAGES

We're almost there. Telling the boys to stick to the plans that had served us so well, and not relenting until the final ball had been bowled.

Jane McGrath Day is now one of the special days of the cricket calendar. As an ambassador for the McGrath Foundation, I will do everything I can to help. Here I shake hands with Glenn as he presents me with my pink cap.

It was nice to take a couple of catches on that last afternoon in Sydney. After tea, we built up an unstoppable momentum.

Saeed Khan/AFP/Getty Images

Saeed Khan/AFP/Getty Images

Images from that last afternoon in Sydney: George Bailey snaring another super catch close-in to end Kevin Pietersen's series, and Michael Carberry with his broken bat. A good bloke, Carberry took it in the right spirit.

Ryan Pierse/Getty Images

It's ours! Celebrating the last wicket with Shane Watson, Brad Haddin and Steve Smith.

That's the urn – or a replica at least, that Shane Warne threw to me on the podium in Sydney. It belonged to a photographer, who had bought it as a souvenir. My hand, holding it, is the real thing!

We will never forget the lap of honour we took with the Ashes urn to thank all our supporters in Sydney. Davey Warner and Brad Haddin were rightly elated. They both had a fantastic series.

The urn returns. Words can't describe it.

Having been there myself, I know how important it is to face up to defeat and use it to motivate yourself. I have no doubt the English players here were fuelling their determination for 2015.

We had a long night in the changing room at the SCG. Very late that night, around midnight, Nathan Lyon led us out onto the pitch for the team song. I got to have a lie-down with my new best friend.

Two days after the series had ended we were still celebrating, on this occasion at the Sydney Opera House to thank our loyal fans. Australian cricket supporters had stuck with us through some barren years, and this victory belonged to them too.

The Allan Border Medal night, at Doltone House in Sydney, was a great opportunity to soak up our achievements during the summer. Kyly was looking amazing, as ever (*top*). I was proud to be Test player of the year along with my fellow award winners Aaron Finch (Twenty20 Player of the Year), George Bailey (One-day Player of the Year) and the deserving Allan Border Medal-winner Mitch Johnson (*bottom*).

to win every match against England remains strong. I could not be happier with the way things swung in our favour after what looked like pretty desperate straits.

From where we began this morning, you would never have thought we could turn this match around so quickly. But it went well from the start. The 40 runs Nathan Lyon and Brad Haddin put on for the last wicket were crucial, because they planted some seeds of doubt among the English and gave us confidence as we took the ball. In a low-scoring game, the difference between a 90-run deficit and a 50-run deficit on the first innings is immense.

Hadds and Lyono had a bit of luck, which would have been all the more annoying for Alastair Cook and his boys. I have been in their position many times, and can remember how frustrating it was on the second morning at Lord's in July when Graeme Swann and Stuart Broad kept us in the field for much longer than we wanted, and all their edges and mishits seemed to go for four. Today, Nathan and Hadds got some nicks through and over the slips cordon, Nathan was backing away to upper-cut the short balls, and all sorts of fun and games were going on as the score mounted up. Nathan even tonked James Anderson high over mid-on for a boundary, which caused some enjoyment in our viewing area. By the time Anderson got Hadds out with a bouncer he edged onto his helmet before it was caught by Jonny Bairstow, Hadds was top-scorer in our total with 65 and now the highest-ever scorer for a wicketkeeper in an Ashes series.

Put it together with his world record for dismissals in the series in England, and he hasn't had such a bad year!

What Hadds's innings showed was that when a batsman goes out and backs himself to play his shots, just puts all the demons out of his head, this pitch is quite manageable. When Cook came out to bat, he decided to back himself against the new ball, and put away some nice drives on both sides of the wicket. He was middling everything. Part of me has wondered if Cook isn't going to come good any day now – he is too good a batsman not to – and I was thinking this might be it.

Before too long, Rhino had to go off to have his foot strapped. He didn't have a serious injury, but blisters were hampering him. I brought Nathan Lyon on early, with the ball only five overs old, as he has been having some success bowling to Cook. Fortunately for us, at the other end Michael Carberry was going through the opposite experience from Cook. It can be bizarre, cricket. One batsman was scoring at better than a run a ball, really clicking, and the other could not get it off the square. At lunch, Cook had scored 41 runs from 46 balls, while Carberry had scored five from 50.

At the break, things were looking grim for us. Watto tried to bowl a couple of overs, but his speed was down in the low 120s. Rhino was struggling with those blisters. We were troubling Carberry, but whenever he nicked the ball it seemed to land just where the fielders were not. And Cook was in top form. The last time England led us on the first innings was at Lord's, and we all know what happened there.

I will do my best to explain how we turned it around after lunch. It didn't start very well. Watto bowled two overs from the Members end, trying his best but labouring with his injury. Cook was able to cut him for two fours in his second over, so I took him off and gave Nathan Lyon a bowl.

I had an interesting chat with Nathan when he first came on. I ran down to ask him what field he wanted set. He said, 'I just want to tie this end down and stop them scoring.' I stopped him and said, 'Nath, your job isn't to tie blokes down, it's to take wickets and help us bowl England out.' I wanted to put more expectation on him and make him think his job has a lot more potential than tying down an end and keeping things quiet. He is a wicket-taking bowler. We all know that. Sometimes he just needs to see how much others believe it before he'll believe it himself.

Meanwhile, Mitch was powering in downwind from the Southern Stand end, giving a lot of bother to both Cook and Carberry. He was pitching it well up, and had a big LBW appeal against Carberry turned down when the left-hander jammed a yorker into his pad. We wanted Mitch to follow the usual plan and attack Cook with balls pitched on the full side of a good length, and Nathan did well in his first over to keep Carberry down that end, enabling Mitch to have a good crack at Cook.

Mitch fired in a searing yorker that Cook only just got his bat down on. The ball was beginning to tail both ways with reverse swing. Mitch's next ball was an out-swinger to the left-hander, and Cook defended it. He was pinned back inside his crease because of Mitch's speed. There was one ball we really wanted to see in that situation, and Mitch delivered: a good-length ball, quite full but not a yorker, that drew Cook out a little and then veered in with some late reverse in-swing. It hit Cook's front pad right in front, and we knew it was out. So did Alastair.

Even though it was just one wicket, our first, that was the major breakthrough. Cook had been batting really well and looking like getting away from us. In another hour, he could have taken the whole match away. But Mitch got him with some absolutely brilliant accurate fast bowling. There are many different dimensions to Mitch's bowling now, and this was another of them.

From there, we suddenly had the momentum. Early on, even though Carberry had had so much trouble scoring, he hadn't needed to panic because Cook had been piling up the runs so quickly at the other end. Now, with Cook gone, Carberry was under the pump. Joe Root came in, and Mitch thought he had him caught behind second ball. Neither Watto nor I appealed, but Hadds and Mitch thought he had nicked it. Root, given out, referred it to the DRS and was reprieved.

Nathan Lyon was pinning the batsmen down from the Members end, and I gave Mitch a break so that Peter Siddle could have a bowl. One more wicket, and he could be fresh for a crack at Kevin Pietersen. He had two overs at Root, but wanted to get Carberry on strike. When he did, he bowled around the wicket, and his first ball arced in and trapped the left-hander LBW. As Carberry walked, Root spoke to him and seemed to suggest he wanted him to appeal, but Carberry was certain he was out, and after a long, difficult struggle against the bowlers he was on his way.

During the afternoon the wind really whipped up from the south, and the batsmen were having a lot of trouble rotating the strike against Lyono. All the more to his credit was that he was pinning them down without any assistance from the wicket, which was offering minimal spin. He compensated by bowling in good areas, getting the ball to drift and drop using the wind, and changing his pace subtly. He was applying what I had said to him earlier about attacking the batsmen, not just containing them. A stiff breeze can be a real weapon for the spin bowler who knows how to use it. Three balls after Carberry was out, Root became so desperate to get off strike against Nathan that he ran for a single after driving the ball firmly to Mitch Johnson at mid-off. With the confidence he is carrying at the moment, you would be a brave man to back yourself against Mitch. He threw down the stumps and Root was clearly short of his ground.

Nath was as excited as the rest of us, as it was his wicket, in a way. The pressure he had put Root under was what had caused the error in judgement. Kevin Pietersen hit a single off the next ball, and then Ian Bell, facing his first delivery, was deceived by the flight and drove Nath straight to Mitch for an easy catch. Mitch might not have picked it up at first, but it hung in the air as if in slow motion and he got his hands up safely. Having taken three wickets in six balls, we were over the moon. We were now down to their lower-middle order, and they were only 130-odd runs ahead of us.

Pietersen and Ben Stokes battled through until tea, keeping us at bay. I replaced Nathan and Sidds with Rhino and Mitch, and there were a few close calls. Stokes let one go that whizzed over the top of his middle stump. During his century in Perth, Stokes was safely leaving balls on length, confident that the bounce would take them over the stumps, but here the bounce is not so reliable. Mitch and Rhino were getting some good reverse swing. I set an in-out on-side field for KP as Mitch zeroed in on his body, with a bat-pad waiting for the fended or inside-edged chance and men on the boundary patrolling for the big hit. As luck had it, Pietersen did play a false stroke, but it was an in-between one, a leading edge that popped into space wide of mid-on. You can only plan for percentages – there is no such thing as a certainty.

At tea, Stokes and Pietersen had stemmed the steady fall of wickets and we were again growing hungry for a breakthrough. England's lead was in the 160s. To be honest, I didn't know, and still don't know, what is a gettable fourth-innings target on this pitch. All I wanted was for it to be as small as possible.

After the resumption, I had Sidds and Nathan bowling in partnership again, and it took four overs for the wicket to come. Nathan tossed one up to Stokes, and he went for a big lofted off-drive. But the ball dropped a fraction into the wind, and he mistimed it. Smithy was waiting halfway between mid-off and long-off. It might have been a bad shot, but Nathan deserves full credit for forcing it.

Pietersen was having his usual dramas against Sidds. We had the now-standard two short mid-wickets in place, and Kevin somehow chipped a ball into the gap between them. In the same over, he edged just short of me at second slip. The struggle between defence and attack has clearly been raging inside Pietersen throughout this match, and he decided this time to go on the offensive, cracking a front-foot pull shot and then a cover drive for two fours in Sidds's next over. We didn't mind him playing his shots, but the two boundaries took the English lead past 200, a reminder that we could not afford to let this partnership with Jonny Bairstow get out of hand. I didn't feel that we had enough runs in the bank to allow us to buy a wicket.

Bairstow also had a plan, which was to hit his way out of trouble. In his first dozen or so balls, he played three scoring shots: two sixes off Nathan over mid-on, and a slog-sweep four. I took Nathan off and did a double change, bringing back Ryan and Mitch. The wind was really picking up now, blowing rubbish across the MCG in a way that you don't often see apart from on those really windy cricket grounds in New Zealand. It also switched direction. This big new gusting change was coming from the north, so I brought Mitch on from the Members end so he could have it blowing over his shoulder.

Pietersen was constantly distracted by pieces of litter blowing around or movements behind the bowler. At one point he backed away just as Mitch was about to bowl, and Mitch, in frustration, chucked the ball down the wicket. In our first innings, by contrast, at one stage when Hadds was batting, a bit of shiny plastic blew across the pitch right in front of him as the bowler was about to deliver. The umpire stepped in and stopped the bowler. Hadds just stood there, ready to face. He hadn't even seen it! But Pietersen was distracted by a succession of things, and Mitch grew exasperated. He exchanged a few words with Pietersen, who did his best to take singles and get off strike. In Mitch's next over, he ripped a very fast ball down to Bairstow outside the off stump and the batsman nicked it. After a building partnership, this was another crucial breakthrough for us.

Rhino was struggling with that blister, which had grown and become more like an ulcer, and he was bowling into the strengthening wind. So after two overs

186

I took him off and brought Nathan back at the Southern Stand end, into the wind. At drinks, England were 223 runs ahead with four wickets in hand. Pietersen was the big danger, and their tail-enders might not have had a good series with the bat so far but they only needed to stick around until stumps and they would be setting us an extremely challenging fourth-innings target. It was a nervous time, but I kept reassuring Nathan about his attacking abilities.

His first over after drinks came up with the goods. Second ball, Tim Bresnan went for a pull shot but inside-edged the ball onto his bails. He was so surprised, he thought Hadds must have knocked the bails off and waited for a replay, but there was no doubt. Then, another three balls into that over, Stuart Broad went to drive a ball that again deceived him in flight, and he edged it. I was thrilled to take the catch that gave Nathan his hundredth Test wicket. I had also taken the catch for his first Test wicket, Kumar Sangakkara in Sri Lanka, in exactly the same way, down low to my left, so there was a nice symmetry in the dismissal of Broad. Nathan has taken his chance in the Australian team with both hands, and now stands near the top rung of Australian finger-spinners throughout history. Hopefully the wickets he took today will help him understand his job in this team. I think he understands it now! If you can deceive batsmen in the air with no spin on that pitch, it shows that you are a world-class bowler.

Pietersen was still there, but so destructive has Mitch been on the tail-enders, it has changed the way England's recognised batsmen have approached the last stages of their innings. Knowing that James Anderson could get out any ball to Mitch, Pietersen decided to throw his bat. He hit Mitch down the ground once, but while trying to put Nathan into the Southern Stand he hit one very high and not quite far enough. Out on the rope, Ryan Harris took yet another of the extremely well-judged outfield catches he has been notable for throughout this summer. Pietersen was another huge wicket for us, and for Nathan, it capped his first five-wicket haul in an innings in Test cricket since his debut in Sri Lanka two years ago.

When Mitch trapped Monty Panesar LBW in the next over, we had pulled off something remarkable. We had taken the last five wickets for six runs. At lunch, England were no wickets down and more than 100 ahead of us. We fought back after lunch, but when Bairstow and Pietersen were going hard this afternoon, England were effectively 5/224, and we were under heavy pressure. Now they were all out, and our target was 231. That is a huge difference, chasing 231 as opposed to 300, and I am hoping it will be a match-winning one. I can't praise our bowlers highly enough. And after so many innings where it has been Mitch, Rhino and Sidds wreaking the havoc, today it was especially pleasing to see Nathan Lyon as the attack leader.

I am very apprehensive about this fourth-innings chase, however. This pitch has not been easy for anyone to bat on, with the exception of Brad Haddin in our first innings. It is going to be really challenging when the ball gets old.

Chris and Davey made a nice, positive start tonight, getting us to 30 runs from the first eight overs. But we are mindful that the new ball is easiest to bat against, and behaving most 'normally' on this wicket. When the ball gets softer and more cut up, it will be reverse swinging and harder to survive, as well as harder to score against. It will be difficult to score the runs tomorrow. That said, I could not be happier with the team's performance today. In a summer of brilliant days, this has been up there with the best, particularly because it has shown our resilience and determination to fight our way back into a game when we were well behind. Now we just have to convert that fightback into a win.

Sunday 29 December. Melbourne.

Well, I certainly did not turn up this morning thinking we would win this Test match by eight wickets. I expected a nervous day and us having to dig deep to get there. Instead, our top three batsmen made it surprisingly convincing.

It was a cool, sunny, breezy morning after the change late yesterday. We knew walking out that the best time to bat would be during the new ball period, and hoped Chris Rogers and David Warner would get off to a good start. One of the keys was to be positive and keep the scoreboard moving. We expected that England's plan would be to squeeze the run rate and bog us down, increasing our nerves and tempting us into poor shot selection.

James Anderson started with a maiden to Chris, but Davey would not be held down, square driving his first ball of the day from Stuart Broad to the boundary. Only 197 to win! It still seemed like a long way away.

Soon Broad produced the chance. In his second over, he bowled an immaculate-length ball to Chris and got the edge. Fortunately for us, it went right between keeper Jonny Bairstow and Alastair Cook at first slip, and they were caught in two minds. Bairstow left it. No doubt expecting it to be the keeper's catch, Cook also left it. Then he grabbed at it after it had gone past Bairstow. He got a hand on it, but it went through and ran off for a boundary. It was so much like when we dropped Joe Root at Lord's and Ian Bell at Trent Bridge. When you are doing it tough, all the fifty-fifties feel like they are running against you.

Chris knocked the next ball over slips for another four, and Broad was taken off. Cook said at his press conference after the game that he wanted to save Broad for when the ball was more roughed-up and he could make the most of the potential for reverse swing.

But I know our boys were happy to see that England's best bowler had been given a rest.

Ben Stokes came on from the Members end, and immediately he created another chance. This time Davey nicked it, and it went straight to Cook. This one also went down. Our dressing room would have had a different feeling, and it could have been a much, much tougher day for us, if England had held on to those chances.

Davey didn't last much longer, feathering a bouncer on the off-side. It wasn't the wrong shot to play, just not quite perfectly executed. But if I had been told our openers would add 64 runs in a chase for 231, I would have happily taken it, so I was pleased with Davey for the way he went about his work.

Any apprehension I had while waiting to bat was taken away by how Chris Rogers and Shane Watson batted in the next hour. Watto was clearly hampered by his groin and calf injuries, but he was solid in defence and not letting Anderson get past his bat. Chris was really blooming, playing a series of beautiful late cuts and drives. The first hour could have been messy for us, but in the second hour our boys took charge. Chris played a cracking hook shot off Anderson in front of square leg to bring up our hundred, one of the best strokes of the Test match. Watto drove Bresnan for two thumping fours, one straight and another through point. He hit the ball so cleanly, on what was still a two-paced wicket, and it was kind of commanding batting that Watto is capable of, really dispiriting for the bowlers.

After bowling Root and Tim Bresnan for a while, Cook brought Broad back and gave Monty Panesar his first bowl of the day. But by then, Bucky and Watto were in full flight, scoring at five an over. By lunch we were 1/143. That second hour had broken the match open for us. After the break, Chris moved quickly to his hundred, bringing it up with a sweetly timed cover drive off Anderson. It was another important innings for him, continuing to give him confidence. He has played good cricket throughout both series, in England and in Australia, and it is nice to see him get such reward in Melbourne in front of his family and friends. He batted doggedly for us in the first innings, but today was a different story, fluent and free-scoring, just what we wished for, dispelling any changing-room nerves. The boys were pumped for him.

We were 200 by the time Chris got out, edging an attempted cut off Panesar. I did not expect this morning that I would be walking out to bat with only 31 runs to win. What a luxury our top three had given us. The pitch still couldn't be trusted, and I went out there to try my best to make sure the job got done. After the way they came back, our boys deserved this to be a crushing win. I did not want to lose late wickets and make it look any less convincing than it was. An eight-wicket win sounds beautiful. Fortunately, while I was keeping the ball out,

Watto was happy to take charge, belting a few fours and finally pushing the winning runs off Panesar through mid-wicket. We were euphoric as we celebrated, both in the middle and in the changing rooms later. We have won three Test matches by bowling England out in the fourth innings, and I feel it has been an important step forward for our confidence to go into a fourth innings with the bat and chase down a target.

Four–nil! It's hard to comprehend. To be honest, if you had told me in November that we would be 4–0 ahead by the end of the year, I would have taken some convincing. As positive as I am, this is more than I was prepared to contemplate.

As for my decision to put England in, I think in sport you are judged on the ultimate result. We dismissed England for 255 in the first innings, which I think is a good enough outcome when you send them in to bat. I was worried, yes, particularly after the first five overs on Boxing Day, when the wicket was not offering as much help to the seamers as I had expected it would. When we didn't bowl them out that day, my disappointment was balanced out by how well we had restricted their run-scoring, and by the time we ran through their tail on day two I was happier. Then, when we fell short in the first innings and England were no wicket for effectively 100 at lunch yesterday and we were looking down the barrel of defeat, it looked like we were in a poor position, which some might have attributed to my decision at the toss. But we fought back, and the way the boys batted today, you could say it was a good decision to be batting last on this wicket.

If you send the opposition in and you lose, you are accountable. If you win, people will say you made the right decision. I did think I would have preferred to bat first, but it has turned out in our favour and I am ecstatic to take the win.

I have just left the changing room after a couple of hours with the team and staff. With the Fifth Test match only four days away, the boys will be taking it easy tonight and not celebrating too hard. After the Sydney Test match, if we get another win there, we can celebrate as hard as we like together for a couple of days. For now, I feel a quiet, mellow sense of satisfaction and relief over what we have done here.

Fourth Test

26–29 December 2013.
Melbourne Cricket Ground.

England (first innings)

Batting		R	B	4	6	SR
AN Cook	c: Clarke b: Siddle	27	47	3	0	57.44
MA Carberry	b: Watson	38	103	6	0	36.89
JE Root	c: Haddin b: Harris	24	82	2	0	29.26
KP Pietersen	b: Johnson	71	161	5	1	44.09
IR Bell	c: Haddin b: Harris	27	98	1	0	27.55
BA Stokes	c: Watson b: Johnson	14	23	1	1	60.86
JM Bairstow	b: Johnson	10	17	0	1	58.82
TT Bresnan	c: Bailey b: Johnson	1	14	0	0	7.14
SCJ Broad	lbw: Johnson	11	16	2	0	68.75
JM Anderson	not out	11	24	1	0	45.83
MS Panesar	b: Lyon	2	16	0	0	12.50
Extras	(7lb, 1w, 1nb, 10b)	19				
Total	10 Wkts, 100 overs	255		2.55 Runs/Over		

Fall of wickets 1-48 (Cook, 16.5 ov), 2-96 (Carberry, 33.6 ov), 3-106 (Root, 42.1 ov), 4-173 (Bell, 72.6 ov), 5-202 (Stokes, 80.3 ov), 6-216 (Bairstow, 84.4 ov), 7-230 (Bresnan, 90.1 ov), 8-231 (Pietersen, 90.5 ov), 9-242 (Broad, 94.2 ov), 10-255 (Panesar, 99.6 ov)

Bowling	O	M	R	W	Econ	SR	Extras
RJ Harris	24	8	47	2	1.95	72	
MG Johnson	24	4	63	5	2.62	28.8	(1w)
PM Siddle	23	7	50	1	2.17	138	(1nb)
NM Lyon	22.2	3	67	1	3.00	134	
SR Watson	6.4	2	11	1	1.65	40	

Australia (first innings)

Batting		R	B	4	6	SR
CJL Rogers	c: Pietersen b: Bresnan	61	171	8	0	35.67
DA Warner	c: Bairstow b: Anderson	9	14	2	0	64.28
SR Watson	c: Bairstow b: Stokes	10	15	2	0	66.66
MJ Clarke	b: Anderson	10	34	0	0	29.41
SPD Smith	c: Bell b: Broad	19	77	3	0	24.67
GJ Bailey	c: Bairstow b: Anderson	0	19	0	0	0.00
BJ Haddin	c: Bairstow b: Anderson	65	68	7	1	95.58
MG Johnson	c: Anderson b: Bresnan	2	30	0	0	6.66
RJ Harris	c: Root b: Broad	6	27	1	0	22.22
PM Siddle	c: Bresnan b: Broad	0	5	0	0	0.00
NM Lyon	not out	18	34	3	0	52.94
Extras	(4lb, 0w, 0nb, 0b)	4				
Total	10 Wkts, 82.2 overs	204		2.47 Runs/Over		

Fall of wickets 1-19 (Warner, 6.3 ov), 2-36 (Watson, 11.2 ov), 3-62 (Clarke, 25.2 ov), 4-110 (Smith, 49.5 ov), 5-112 (Rogers, 52.1 ov), 6-122 (Bailey, 57.5 ov), 7-151 (Johnson, 66.2 ov), 8-162 (Harris, 71.6 ov), 9-164 (Siddle, 73.3 ov), 10-204 (Haddin, 82.2 ov)

Bowling	O	M	R	W	Econ	SR	Extras
JM Anderson	20.2	4	67	4	3.29	30.5	
SCJ Broad	20	6	45	3	2.25	40	
BA Stokes	15	4	46	1	3.06	90	
TT Besnan	18	6	24	2	1.33	54	
MS Panesar	9	2	18	0	2.00	–	

England (second innings)

Batting		R	B	4	6	SR
AN Cook	lbw: Johnson	51	64	7	0	79.68
MA Carberry	lbw: Siddle	12	81	1	0	14.81
JE Root	run out (Johnson)	15	24	1	0	62.50
KP Pietersen	c: Harris b: Lyon	49	90	6	0	54.44
IR Bell	c: Johnson b: Lyon	0	1	0	0	0.00
BA Stokes	c: Smith b: Lyon	19	55	1	0	34.54
JM Bairstow	c: Haddin b: Johnson	21	28	2	2	75.00
TT Bresnan	b: Lyon	0	8	0	0	0.00
SCJ Broad	c: Clarke b: Lyon	0	3	0	0	0.00
JM Anderson	not out	1	6	0	0	16.66
MS Panesar	lbw: Johnson	0	6	0	0	0.00

Extras	(6lb, 0w, 0nb, 5b)	11		
Total	10 Wkts, 61 overs	179		2.93 Runs/Over

Fall of wickets 1-65 (Cook, 21.3 ov), 2-86 (Carberry, 27.5 ov), 3-86 (Root, 28.2 ov), 4-87 (Bell, 28.4 ov), 5-131 (Stokes, 44.5 ov), 6-173 (Bairstow, 54.3 ov), 7-174 (Bresnan, 57.2 ov), 8-174 (Broad, 57.5 ov), 9-179 (Pietersen, 59.4 ov), 10-179 (Panesar, 61 ov)

Bowling	O	M	R	W	Econ	SR	Extras
RJ Harris	10	1	34	0	3.40	–	
MG Johnson	15	5	25	3	1.66	30	
NM Lyon	17	3	50	5	2.94	30.4	
PM Siddle	15	6	46	1	3.06	90	
SR Watson	4	2	13	0	3.25	–	

Australia (second innings)

Batting		R	B	4	6	SR
CJL Rogers	c: Bairstow b: Panesar	116	155	13	0	74.83
DA Warner	c: Bairstow b: Stokes	25	47	2	0	53.19
SR Watson	not out	83	90	11	0	92.22
MJ Clarke	not out	6	20	1	0	30.00
SPD Smith						
GJ Bailey						
BJ Haddin						
MG Johnson						
PM Siddle						
RJ Harris						
NM Lyon						

Extras	(0lb, 0w, 1nb, 0b)	1		
Total	2 Wkts, 51.5 overs	231		4.45 Runs/Over

Fall of wickets 1-64 (Warner, 17.6 ov), 2-200 (Rogers, 45.5 ov)

Bowling	O	M	R	W	Econ	SR	Extras
JM Anderson	11	2	26	0	2.36	–	
SCJ Broad	10	0	58	0	5.80	–	
MS Panesar	7.5	0	41	1	5.23	47	
BA Stokes	12	0	50	1	4.16	72	(1nb)
JE Root	4	1	8	0	2.00	–	
TT Bresnan	7	1	48	0	6.85	–	

6

THE FIFTH
TEST MATCH

Monday 30 December. **Melbourne to Sydney.**

Today was a well-earned day off for all the boys. The
Sydney players returned home quite tired from the Test
match in Melbourne and looking forward to a good
night's sleep. The others could either stay in Melbourne
or do as they pleased before the team meets up again in
our team hotel in Sydney tomorrow.

As soon as I got home, I dropped my stuff at the
house and then met Duncan Kerr at the gym to train for
an hour and a half. Then I hopped in the car and drove to
Steve's practice at Beecroft for some time on the MedX
again. I thought I needed some strength training for my
mind as much as anything else, and the back treatment as
a precautionary measure.

199

Tuesday 31 December. **Sydney.**

New Year's Eve in Sydney is always a special time, no more so than when we are enjoying such a fabulous summer. Today has been pretty busy for me, actually, and I will be going to bed before the midnight fireworks.

First thing this morning, I drove from home in Bondi back to Beecroft for some more work with my physio Steve. My neck has been stiff for a little while now, and I had my back looked at. It's going okay, touch wood, but I still spent some more time on the MedX machine for regular maintenance.

From there I drove to the team hotel, the Quay West in the Rocks, where the boys arrived around 1.00 pm. We had recovery, rehab and medical screenings. Then I had Kunal Sharma, the owner of Spartan Sporting Goods, sit with me for three hours at the hotel, changing the stickers on my bats. Spartan put a new range out each year and it has become our tradition after Christmas to have the stickers refreshed. Normally Kunal takes my bats away to have them re-stickered, but this time we did it together and had a nice long chat.

My bats look great, and have a McGrath Foundation sticker on them as well for this Test match, which is played in honour of the late Jane McGrath and as a fund-raiser for breast cancer research and care. Kyly and I are ambassadors of the foundation. I am a huge fan and friend of Glenn McGrath, so anything I can do to help, I will.

This evening, in keeping with our team tradition, our manager Gavin Dovey organised a separate room in the Quay West with a balcony where the team could gather with their partners and children to have dinner and drinks together and watch the fireworks and other New Year's Eve celebrations at Circular Quay. It's a fantastic box seat to enjoy the fireworks from. Kyly and I stayed for the first fireworks, and then left at around 9.30 pm. It's not a compulsory event for Sydney-based players, who are free to celebrate with their families. We have decided to stay in the hotel rather than at home, and I am going to be asleep by 10.30 pm. We can save our big celebration for the end of the series. But for tonight, it was great to see everyone with their kids and families, feeling laidback, enjoying the night together. Tomorrow I will be up first thing. I'm looking forward to seeing the SCG wicket.

Wednesday 1 January. Sydney.

New Year's Day! How fast has 2013 gone? It's amazing when you consider how much cricket we have played this year, how much drama there has been, how much travelling, how many sessions and matches and press conferences and training and physio treatments and everything else – yet it seems like yesterday that we were here at the SCG preparing for our Test match against Sri Lanka. This past year will take quite a while to sink in.

My favourite week of the year? The Sydney Test match. My favourite ground? The Sydney Cricket Ground. My favourite place? Home. I love preparing for my home Test and playing in Sydney. My family and friends will be here, and I am so proud to be leading Australia in front of them.

The team and support staff gathered for our photo at the SCG, and while the rest of us did our normal training in the nets and fielding, the bowlers did recovery with our strength and conditioning coach, Damien Mednis. It is so important in these back-to-back Test match weeks that the bowlers are looked after and patched up so they can keep going. Everyone is a little worse for wear after four Test matches in not much more than a month. Watto's calf and groin are still not 100 per cent. Ryan Harris's right knee is requiring attention and he has a blister that looks pretty gross. But considering all the Test cricket he has missed in the past, you would also not want to be the person standing between him and playing in this match. Nothing will stop him.

At training, I took a close look at the SCG ground staff's wicket, which is a lot greener than expected. Last year, against Sri Lanka, I bowled first here after winning the toss. This time could be similar. But there are still two days until the Test match, so we'll see how it turns out after some sunshine.

Both of the teams and their support staff went to the Prime Minister's official residence at Kirribilli this afternoon for a couple of hours, bringing their families and kids. The day ran pretty smoothly, and I am extremely grateful to Mr and Mrs Abbott for having us. We had plenty of photos taken, and it was nice to catch up with various people whom I don't see very often.

I am staying at home tonight. It's so nice to stay in your own bed, have your own shower, and sit on your own couch. Kyly's cooking dinner at the moment and I'm sitting on the couch with our dogs: my Staffordshire bull terrier, Jerry, and Kyly's Pomeranian, Poochy. These are the simple things I miss when I'm away so much. I sit here and think, life doesn't get much better.

Thursday 2 January. Sydney.

Today we had our last training session before the Test match. Everyone in the playing group went down to the SCG, even though it was optional. That's a great indicator of our team spirit at the moment: everyone wants to play and train.

It has been a nice, hot day. After some rain overnight, there was steam coming off the ground. The SCG always feels different from Melbourne at this time of year, more humid, almost tropical.

I took another look at the wicket, and have some concerns. I don't think I have ever seen this much grass on an SCG wicket in my time for New South Wales or Australia. It's extremely green! I'm not sure what they were thinking. I'm looking forward to seeing it tomorrow after it has had some more sunshine on it, and another mow and roll and some drying out. That might turn it a bit whiter. At least, that's what all of the batsmen are hoping for. Either way, both teams have to play on it. We will assess it in the morning and I can make a decision about batting or bowling first if I win another toss. But surely Alastair Cook is due to win one. (A toss, I mean!)

As for the team make-up, I am waiting on the selectors' final choice. They brought Tasmania's young batsman Alex Doolan and the Western Australian fast bowler Nathan Coulter-Nile into a 14-man squad for this Test match, but today they announced that they were releasing Alex and Nathan back to their States, so we are back to the same twelve we have had for all five Test matches. In my entire career, Australia has never fielded the same eleven for a five-match series.

I have heard about three different selection possibilities. One is for James Faulkner, whose thumb has recovered since it got hit in the nets in Perth, to come in for George Bailey, as cover in case Shane Watson can't bowl his full complement of overs. There is also some talk, considering how green and grassy the wicket is, of bringing in Faulkner as an extra fast bowler instead of Nathan Lyon. And there is also the chance of us retaining the same team, which would be very special for all eleven guys. In any case, I will hear what the selectors have to say once we get to the ground and assess the wicket tomorrow.

Friday 3 January. **Sydney.**

When I got to the SCG this morning, I have to say the wicket still looked quite poor for the first day of a Test match. That makes our comeback this afternoon all the more meritorious.

I said it yesterday, but even after it was mown today I will repeat my opinion that I have never seen so much grass on an SCG wicket for a Test match. I am more than a little surprised, considering how much time they had to prepare. We have had good weather in Sydney leading up to the game, so I am bemused that we turn up and see so much grass on the track. The wicket is quite dry underneath, but the parallel stripes of darker and lighter grass suggest that there are corrugations that will produce uneven pace and bounce. It just doesn't look like a good Test-match wicket to me, which is disappointing.

If I won the toss, I was going to bowl. Definitely. It wasn't like Melbourne where I was caught in about five minds. No question, if I won the toss I was going to bowl.

Alastair won, for the first time in the series. He wanted to bowl too. I think we both looked at the wicket and thought the same thing.

In our changing room, we all knew it would be a nasty wicket to bat on before lunch, and that we would need a lot of luck. We lost four wickets in the session, which, considering the state of the wicket, was quite a good result.

It was an overcast morning, quite muggy but not as hot as the past few days. We went into the match with the same eleven, the first time not only in my career but in all Ashes history, I am told, that the same team has played in every Test of a five-match series. That is a credit to the players' form and determination, of course, but also to the efforts of the support staff, from Doc Peter Brukner and team physio Alex Kountouris, who has so often gone above and beyond the call of duty, in patching the guys up to keep us all going. I can also pay my respects to Steve, my physio when I'm in Sydney and not on the road with Alex, for his work with me, and my personal trainer Duncan Kerr.

England, meanwhile, were taking the field with three players who were not only new to their team on this tour but new to Test cricket. They brought a 17-man squad and have now chosen 18 players in the Ashes series. Boyd Rankin is a tall fast bowler in the Chris Tremlett mode and we had played against him before in the one-day series in England. Gary Ballance, a left-hander who also played against us in England, has come in for Joe Root, which surprised us all. Some of the English press had been touting Root as a successor to Alastair Cook as captain – not at some point in the distant future, but immediately – and now Root is not even in the team. They have also omitted Monty Panesar in favour of Scott Borthwick, a leg-spinning all–rounder. It is stunning to step back for a minute and think that those familiar faces from the England team, such as Jonathan Trott, Root, Matt Prior, Tim Bresnan and Graeme Swann, are no longer in their team. But it also provides us with a challenge, as we have to devise new plans against opponents we don't know too much about.

We did well in the first hour, losing only one wicket. David Warner made a nice positive start but got a good ball from Stuart Broad. Chris Rogers and Shane Watson kept things going during that difficult hour, though, and by the first drinks break we were feeling confident that the worst of the conditions were behind us and we could set sail for a big first innings.

It was not to be. Three overs after drinks, Chris misjudged a short ball and pulled it down, through his legs, onto his stumps. I was out there at 2/51, and facing a tough period before lunch. I got off the mark first ball with a push through cover, but found it difficult to judge the pace and bounce of the wicket. My footwork was apprehensive but I was concentrating hard. Rotating the strike is always an answer to the challenge, but I nearly got myself out when I took a single off Broad in front of point and Michael Carberry picked it up cleanly and took a shy at the stumps I was running to. If he had hit, I think I might have been out.

Broad and Rankin were testing me out with a lot of short balls, but I got a pull shot away off Broad and felt a little better. It was tough, though, and I never felt I could trust the pitch. Ben Stokes came on from the Paddington end, replacing Rankin. I played out a maiden against Broad. Then Stokes bowled me a pretty good length ball outside off stump. With every chance that the ball could move in off the wicket, I had to play at it, and got a thick outside edge which Ian Bell caught at second slip. It is the type of thing that can happen when you are sent in to bat on a grassy and uneven first-morning wicket. It was disappointing when I was so excited about playing at home, and I felt that I had left the team in trouble at 3/78.

Watto and Steve Smith continued to play in a positive manner, however, and we looked like we were going to lunch at three wickets down. In the conditions, you would say that that would have been a great position for us. But on the third-last ball of the session, Anderson ducked one in to Watto and trapped him LBW. It is to Watto's credit that he has made adjustments to avoid this form of dismissal since our tour of England, but in bowler-friendly circumstances Anderson got him this time. It left us 4/94 at lunch and in a tight spot.

We were soon five down when Broad got George Bailey, but when Brad Haddin went out and cracked a couple of beautiful drives, it looked possible that the old marvel might do it again. People have commented that the top order can't keep relying on Hadds to cover up for our failings, and obviously that is true, but a cricket team is not just a list of individuals; when it's playing well, it is a unit whose parts are fitting together and playing for each other. I don't think you will hear Hadds complaining that he has to salvage a mess left by the top-order batsmen. He loves going out to bat with a job to do. We would love it if we scored so many runs up the top that he never even had to bat, but in cricket you will often get good bowlers on difficult pitches who take early wickets. If your team is going well, everyone down the order will be contributing in some way, if needed.

A good example of that is Smithy, who was batting confidently alongside Hadds. Smithy will be the first to say that he was disappointed in his contributions before the Perth Test match. But when we really needed him, in Perth and here in Sydney, he stepped up. When we really needed Hadds, he stepped up too. That's what being in a team means.

Today, Hadds started more slowly than usual. He had to defend very straight and put up with a peppering of short balls. When he was facing Broad, he was batting deeper in his crease than usual, to cope with the short stuff. When the English saw him doing that and pitched the ball up more, he was quickly onto his front foot to drive as crisply as always.

He had a big appeal against him when he was on nine. It was an LBW appeal off Anderson at first, but the wicketkeeper caught the ball so they were going up for an inside edge as well. The umpire gave Hadds not out, and England referred it to the DRS. The replay showed no inside edge and no LBW, so he was fine.

Broad and Anderson bowled well after lunch, and it was all Hadds and Smithy could do to keep them out. There were plenty of plays and misses, and Smithy was often letting the ball go only to get struck on the inside of his thigh. But once Broad and Anderson were taken off and replaced by Stokes and Rankin, you could see the pressure ease. There were more balls just short of a length, and not quite the same relentless accuracy. It was almost drinks before Smithy played his first attacking shot after lunch, a cut over point off Rankin. Hadds was also seeing the ball better now.

At the drinks break, I think they realised that with a pitch so variable in bounce and pace, and quicker than Melbourne, sooner or later a delivery was going to have their name on it. So, in typical style, Hadds and Smithy decided to counter-attack. In the hour before those mid-session drinks, they scored 35 runs. In the next hour, they piled on 70. It was courageous cricket, but that is the way we like to play. Hadds hit Stokes for three fours in an over straight after drinks, in the full arc between point and mid-wicket. Smithy got hit on the hand by one that jumped, but then flayed a square drive to the fence. It was a great spectacle, with both sides attacking each other and desperate to gain the upper hand.

Late that session, things became difficult for England. Scott Borthwick came on, but found it hard to find a testing length. Smithy hit a full toss for four in Borthwick's first over to bring up his thousandth Test run, a great achievement for the young fellow and the first of many such milestones, I hope.

Then Rankin pulled up sore. It looked like a hamstring, and he went off after one ball. England were now going to have to rely heavily on Anderson, Broad and Stokes. At least the wicket was conducive to fast bowling today, but it might hurt them later in the match.

After tea, as the English bowlers began to get tired and bowled a little too short, Hadds took full toll, blazing boundaries all around the ground. It was another amazing innings, and looked like a definite hundred until, out of nowhere, he edged Stokes and was out for 75. Scoring at least a half-century in five straight Test matches is unprecedented for a wicketkeeper in an Ashes series, and nobody could deserve such a record more than our outstanding vice-captain.

His dismissal was a reminder that the pitch still held quite a few surprises. As the sun came out in the afternoon, the wicket improved, but there is enough grass on it to offer plenty of seam movement and some spin.

After Hadds was out, Smithy took over. England were not bouncing him as they had in Perth, so he didn't have many opportunities to play his pull shot, but his driving was safe and clinical. Half an hour into the session, Rankin surprised everyone by coming back on and starting another over, but again he pulled up and had to go off. It was thought to be a hamstring, but since play ended England have said it was cramps. It is not a complete shock that he would be struggling for fitness, having not played much first-class cricket all tour and then being asked to come into a demanding Test match.

England tried to do a Johnson and Harris to Mitch Johnson and Ryan Harris, when they came in to partner Smithy, bowling short-pitched balls from over and around the wicket. It only had limited success. Mitch survived the bouncers but gave his wicket away trying to slog Borthwick, while Ryan hit an Anderson bouncer out of the ground before driving a full-length ball from Stokes to short cover. Peter Siddle was out first ball, and Stokes got his third wicket for the over when Smithy slapped a catch to mid-on.

It was a wonderful innings by Smithy, another hundred, his third in the past six Test matches. I would have been happy with any team score more than 250 after being sent in, and would have been delighted with 250 after we were 5/97. So to get 326, and to do it so quickly, was a great effort by Steve and Brad in particular.

I am hoping the wicket will quicken up tomorrow with more sun on it. Late today, we had six overs at England, and Mitch and Rhino bowled with real fire.

Mitch in particular looked like getting a wicket every ball. In Mitch's second over, I moved Nathan Lyon to a wideish leg slip. I have used a catcher in that position throughout the series, and felt that it might put a second thought in the batsman's mind about playing balls off his ribs. We have studied Carberry at length, and he has a habit of fending short balls off his hip or ribs in the air behind square leg. The angle of Mitch's delivery, when he comes around the wicket, is particularly awkward for a left-hander playing this kind of shot, as the ball almost feels like it's coming from behind the batsman's leading shoulder. Throughout the series, it has always been a matter of getting the placement right, and bowling the right ball. But you can't overdo it, because then you are giving the batsman a lot of leg-side runs. The ball has to come as a surprise, and be perfectly directed, and the fieldsman has to be in just the right place.

Within two deliveries, the move had paid a dividend. Mitch got one up into Carberry's armpit, and he parried it with his glove and bat handle. It lobbed just wide of Nathan, but he dived to his right and snared a superb catch. When things are going well for you, it sometimes seems like you can do no wrong. This was one of those dismissals that gave our team a new injection of self-belief.

James Anderson came out as night-watchman, and managed to get through to stumps. We feel like we have ended the day on top, after spending much of it on the back foot. If that wicket does quicken up as we suspect it might, and we bowl the right length, we might get a few nicks. Hope so!

Saturday 4 January. **Sydney.**

Talk about the game moving forward. Today we saw an exceptional performance once again by our bowlers. At one stage I thought we might bowl England out for less than 100, and if we had done that I certainly would have sent them in again. But as it turned out, we have had to bat again. All the same, I wouldn't be at all surprised if the match is over tomorrow.

It was one of those exhilarating days for us, and for the big crowd watching. The weather was much warmer and sunnier than yesterday. Ryan Harris started from the Paddington end, and he did what he has done so often, which is to find the danger zone first-up, when batsmen want it least. Alastair Cook is very good at leaving the ball early in his innings, but the first ball he got from Rhino was a straight, fast delivery that he had to defend, and the second started outside off stump but swung into him. He left it, and it was plumb LBW.

That incredible start could have got even better the next ball. Rhino bowled a beauty to Ian Bell, who had moved up the order to number three due to Joe Root's omission. Bell had to play at it, and a regulation edge flew to Shane Watson at first slip. Watto is an excellent slips catcher, but this one went down.

Still, our tails were up. Bell got a leading edge to the last ball of the over, and it nearly carried to Peter Siddle at mid-on. It looked like the pitch was going to help the fast bowlers, and our 326 was feeling like about 500.

James Anderson was still there, as night-watchman, and tried his best against the short balls. England's tail-enders have looked like they haven't wanted to be out there against Mitch, in particular, ever since Brisbane, but Anderson got behind the line and risked injury. He was hit on the hands a few times and required the physio to come out and treat him. The short ball might have made him uncomfortable, but it was the full off-stump ball that got him out, when he played forward to Mitch and nicked one to me at second slip.

Next over, Rhino thought he had Bell LBW. We were a bit uncertain about referring it, and, as per our usual process, Rhino left it to Hadds and me. Maybe a little fired up by the occasion, we referred it, but the replay showed it clearly missing leg stump. We had got it wrong. It wasn't a great referral, as it turned out when we examined the replay closely.

Kevin Pietersen had come in at the fall of Anderson's wicket, and he looked unimpressed with the pitch. He played a shot at nearly every ball, and was soon on his way, nicking Rhino to first slip, where this time Watto made no mistake.

Gary Ballance came out and looked very composed. Bell, meanwhile, was working hard to defend and find the same concentration he had had in England. That series, in which he scored three centuries, is too recent for us to forget how much he can hurt us. He remains a quality batsman, even if he hasn't had the series in Australia that he would have wanted. He worked and worked, and saw off Ryan and Mitch. I brought on Sidds and Watto, and they fell into their usual disciplined roles. They have barely bowled a bad ball, let alone a bad spell, all summer. It has been great to watch from second slip. Sidds just nagged and nagged at Bell until he got one in the perfect area, bail-height, fourth-stump line, in the last over before drinks. Bell played forward correctly enough, but nicked it to Hadds.

With England 5/23, we were feeling so irresistible that I would certainly have asked them to follow on if I had the option. Putting myself in their shoes, I would have hated to go out and bat again on that wicket so soon after the first innings. But after the first drinks break of the day, Ballance and Ben Stokes played some good cricket, though Stokes was lucky when he inside-edged Sidds and the replay showed it had bounced a centimetre or two before Hadds caught it.

I brought Mitch on for an over from the Paddington end, but immediately switched him back to the Randwick end where he had bowled his first spell. He felt that the breeze had changed direction, and was into his face when he was coming from the Paddington end.

Immediately, he hit Ballance in the helmet, which caused a long delay just before lunch, and we lost about two overs. That meant England got through to the break without losing another wicket, and our chances of enforcing the follow-on – we needed to bowl them out for 126 or less – were receding.

The dryness underneath the surface of the wicket has offered some potential for the spin bowlers, especially one like Nathan Lyon who bowls in the upper 80–90 kilometres per hour range. After lunch, I had Nathan bowling from the Randwick end and Mitch from the Paddington end. With his fifth ball, Nathan struck, a classic off-spinner's wicket, the left-handed Ballance pushing forward defensively and getting an outside edge.

The wicket was fiery, with a bouncer from Mitch taking off and clearing Hadds for four byes, but it wasn't just the wicket. When Mitch bowled a yorker to Stokes and just about broke his foot, it had nothing to do with the pitch, the ball was just too fast for the batsman. Mitch has sustained this pace and hostility for five straight Test matches now, in all varieties of weather and atmospheric conditions, on some very diverse pitches. He was as hostile and pacy today as he was in Brisbane. What a spearhead he has been.

With Jonny Bairstow in, I replaced Nathan with Sidds at the Randwick end. Again though, the breeze shifted, so I brought Nathan back and switched Sidds to the Paddington end to replace Mitch.

I gave Sidds and Nathan a fairly long spell in partnership. Stokes and Bairstow played stoutly, and I will pay credit to them for their resistance. Sometimes it helps to be young, with nothing to lose. We thought we had Stokes LBW to Nathan and went for a referral, but it was missing the stumps again, so I had lost both of our referrals.

The young English pair lasted for more than an hour before Sidds broke through. Bairstow plays with quite a strong bottom hand, and on a pitch with such variable bounce I thought it was worth having our so-called 'man on the wicket' at silly mid-on, closer to the umpire than the batsman. About an over and a half after I put him there, Bairstow gave him a catch. It was a great reward for Sidds after a longish spell in the draining heat and humidity, and he followed it up, on the last ball of the over, with a perfect top-of-off delivery that Stokes let go. You have to be good to draw a misjudgement from a batsman who has been out there for nearly two and a half hours, but Sidds did that, knocking off the bail on its way through. Exceptional bowling.

After Sidds finished his six-over spell, Rhino came back from the Paddington end and immediately struck, getting Scott Borthwick to nick an attempted drive. By then, England were one run from avoiding the follow-on, and we only had to dismiss Stuart Broad or Boyd Rankin, the last pair.

Earlier, it had looked like we might bowl England out within 40 overs, but now we had bowled more than 50. I am not sure what I would have done if we had taken the wicket but Rankin made it a moot point by hitting Nathan Lyon down the ground and getting them past the follow-on, so we knew we would be batting again by the time Mitch bowled Rankin a few overs later.

A late flurry of hitting from Broad had whittled our lead down to 171, but we felt we had a clear advantage in the match. Our messages, at the change of innings, were simple. Be positive! Get them before they get you!

Davey and Chris began with a volley of fours all around the ground. On this type of wicket, you never know what Davey will do. He could as easily have been the bloke to knock up a quick hundred as to get a duck. As it turned out, when he was on 16 he got a good ball from Anderson that trapped him on the crease and he was LBW. Watto also went out and played positively, but after crunching a couple of boundaries he edged Anderson for Bairstow to take a very good catch, leaping across with his right glove in front of first slip.

Going in at 2/47, I did my best to play straight and with positive intent, and felt good driving Anderson straight. Shortly after that, an unusual thing happened. Chris got a thick edge on a drive and the ball ran down to third man. We ran three, and the throw came in to Bairstow. He thought he might catch Chris napping at the non-striker's end, so he pelted the ball at the stumps there.

It missed, and nobody was backing up, so it scooted away for four overthrows. Chris and Peter Siddle are the two Australian batsmen not to have hit a six during this series – but Chris is the only one to get a seven!

Anderson and Broad were bowling well and I couldn't help sympathising with the English batsmen who had to face our bowlers on this wicket. Anderson got one past me, and the next over I pushed at Broad outside the off stump and nicked it. The wicket is very two-paced, maybe three- or four-paced, and this one sped up noticeably off the deck. I have not had a good Test match with the bat, which is acutely disappointing.

Steve Smith was unable to repeat his first-innings heroics with the bat, but in the final half-hour of play Chris Rogers and George Bailey put on a nice little partnership that sets them up well for tomorrow. Chris in particular was outstanding, scoring 73 not out without any apparent concern aside from one ball that leapt up and hit him on the finger. As in Melbourne, and at Chester-le-Street in England, Chris has saved his best innings for the toughest batting surfaces.

In my opinion, what we are playing on this week is probably unacceptable for Test cricket. For the last couple of years, the Sydney Cricket Ground wicket hasn't been great. The SCG is one of my favourite grounds, if not my very favourite, and of course it is my home ground, so it is all the more disheartening when we are not provided with a wicket that is up to scratch for an Ashes contest.

This game is moving forward so fast, I can't see how it won't be over tomorrow, as long as we bowl as well as we have and keep on holding our catches. The cricket is no doubt entertaining to watch, but I wonder how happy the authorities will be with a Test match that falls well short of going the five-day distance.

In any case, tomorrow is going to be a very big day. I hope the rain stays away, and allows us to have a big celebration on Jane McGrath Day.

Sunday 5 January. Sydney.

Yes! Wow, what a day, what a summer. I can't believe it. I was stunned when we won back the Ashes within three Test matches, but if you had told me back in November that *this*, a whitewash, would happen, I would have thought, *Dream on*.

Today went perfectly to plan. In cricket, we don't often get days like this, so we soak it up when it happens. Tomorrow can't be taken for granted.

As if to give us a sign that nothing can be taken for granted in anyone's future, and that cricket is only a game and not a matter of life and death, today's play commemorated the late Jane McGrath. Before the start of play, Glenn McGrath presented us and the English team with specially made pink caps. The whole Sydney Cricket Ground was decked out in pink, with the public from both nations getting right behind the fund-raising effort. From the field, it makes for a great sight. Later today, we all signed a Test shirt and presented it to the McGrath Foundation to auction off for fund-raising. Jane was a wonderful, strong woman, and our whole team stands right behind everything the foundation does.

The poet Rupert McCall came into our changing room before play, and read the Ashes poem he had just finished. He's an amazing poet and a very well-spoken man. For me personally, having always cared greatly about the history of the game, I found it an emotion-charged reading. Rupert's poem goes right back to the inception of the Ashes in 1882 and takes in some great Australian and English players all the way to the present day. It was really lovely and inspiring for us to listen to.

The weather was more humid than the past couple of days, with clouds hovering about suggesting the possibility of rain. A Sydney Test match rarely gets by without a bit of moisture.

Chris Rogers and George Bailey, two guys in their thirties who were not in the Australian team when we were playing here a year ago, made a steady beginning to the day against James Anderson and Stuart Broad. Both of them drove some nice boundaries, and they outlasted the first bowling partnership.

Ben Stokes came on and, for his first bowl in the series, Kevin Pietersen. Kevin is a useful off-spinner, but it probably asks questions about England's selection when Pietersen is given the first turn of the day in the spin department on the Sydney Cricket Ground. He bowled quite well, too.

Bucky moved calmly to 99, and then nearly ran himself out trying to steal a second run off Pietersen. George sent him back, one of the benefits of experience. A few balls later, Chris waited for the loose ball and cut it away behind point for his second hundred in Australia and his third in Tests. This innings was his hundredth half-century in first-class cricket, which underscores the mountains of runs he has made on both sides of the world in a career that started before mine. It was terrific to see him make another hundred, and sets him up with great confidence for the challenges ahead in South Africa.

Chris and George lasted until the first drinks break. George has put the team first whenever he has batted this summer, and again he went on the attack even though he probably felt under some pressure for his place. He eventually holed out to deep square leg, but as always his quick scoring advanced our cause.

Our lower order fell away in a bit of a hurry, as all the boys went out there to amass some quick runs. We were confident that we had enough on the board, and by the time we were all out for 276 we were energised and geed up to bowl. It has been such a great summer when we have been in the field, and it felt very special indeed to be gathering together to do it one last time. We wanted to go out there and do justice to the standards we have maintained since Brisbane.

Rhino started from the Paddington end and Mitch from the Randwick end, and they were both immediately up to full pace. Their accuracy has been astonishing, and it only took six balls for Mitch to break through. He bowled a full ball on a fourth- or fifth-stump line to Alastair Cook, who felt for it and feathered a catch. It was such a fine edge that Watto didn't hear it, but I did and I was racing up to embrace Mitch. It was another cast-iron example of our bowlers following their plans.

Ian Bell was many observers' choice to bat at number three ever since Jonathan Trott left the England team, but they went with Joe Root in the previous Tests and it has obviously been hard for Bell to come into the role on a tough wicket in the last Test match. I replaced Rhino with Peter Siddle, and three overs later brought Rhino back at the Randwick end to replace Mitch. Bell went after him, upper-cutting a six, but then tried to dab a late cut fine of gully, only succeeding in hitting a catch to David Warner. It probably tells the story of Bell's year. In England, on their slow wickets, he scored what seemed like thousands of runs with that shot. In Australia, we haven't given him the same opportunities, and when we have, he has found it difficult to control the ball the way he did at home.

By drinks, Kevin Pietersen had joined Michael Carberry and we were feeling that we were creating enough chances to bring us the last eight wickets today. A funny thing happened just after drinks, when Carberry played an orthodox defensive shot to Ryan Harris. The ball hit his bat high on the splice, and the bat just snapped. It was only held together by the sticker. Carberry had a bit of a laugh and pretended to throw his bat to the ground in anger. I have seen bats break, but I've never seen one break like that before, like it had been hit with a sledgehammer. The moment felt symbolic, in a way, of a summer in which very fast bowling has played a decisive role; but Carberry, a good bloke, took it in the right humour.

Carberry was batting well, but Pietersen didn't last much longer, inside-edging Rhino onto his thigh. The ball looked like it was lobbing over George Bailey's head at bat-pad, but he stepped back, his eyes in the sun, flung up a hand and came down with a terrific catch.

In the 15th over, I brought on Nathan Lyon from the Paddington end. If this game had been tighter and had gone into the fourth or fifth days, I would have been interested to see Nathan go to work on this grassy but turning wicket. With his first ball, we thought he had Carberry out. Hadds, who took the catch, and George Bailey at short leg were convinced that Carberry had edged it. I wasn't sure, and nor was Nathan, but we referred it on Hadds's insistence. The replay said it was not out. One area we haven't been very good at in this Test match is our DRS referrals.

Fortunately, it hasn't affected the outcome. When we were losing Test matches in England, there was a lot of scrutiny and criticism of the number of unsuccessful DRS referrals we made. I don't know if we have been better or worse in this area of the game here in Australia, but because we are winning the Test matches, the issue has passed more or less without comment.

Gary Ballance again showed some steadiness, and he and Carberry got them through to tea. Even though we still had to take seven wickets, recent history shows that we can get them quickly, and we took our break thinking a result today was possible yet. It had become a beautiful sunny afternoon, the ground was packed, and emotionally we wanted to finish it off in front of all those supporters.

Mitch started the new session from the Randwick end. He was straight up to full pace and accuracy, and within two balls he set things in motion, drawing Carberry into a defensive stroke which he edged to Hadds. Six to go!

It was also fitting that the last collapse of this Ashes series should be triggered by Mitch. Three balls later, he rifled one through Ballance and trapped him in front. No referrals; it was going to hit middle and middle. Five to go.

You could feel the momentum building, like an earthquake around the ground. We were unstoppable. Four balls into his first over from the Paddington end,

Nathan Lyon induced an inside edge from Jonny Bairstow, and it was taken, via a deflection off the pad, by George Bailey. It squirted quickly through the air, and he took another of the several very good catches he has snared in that position during the series. Four to go.

On the last ball of that same over, Nathan squared up the left-handed Scott Borthwick, a dream off-spinner's wicket, the edge flying low to my left. I just moved instinctively, and found the ball had stuck in my fingertips. The boys were getting very excited now. Three to go.

In two overs since tea, we had taken four wickets. Twelve balls, four wickets. We knew that England must have been talking about stopping their habit of losing wickets in clusters, because we have been through the same thing just a short few Test matches ago. When it happens, you feel so helpless, and a sense of despair falls over the changing room. I have spoken for a long time about the importance of momentum in cricket, and today was another example. Against good bowling attacks, when they get momentum up it can be very, very hard to stop them with the bat – as we found at times in England. Today, it was our turn to be the team that had its tail up, and England's turn to feel overwhelmed.

Ben Stokes and Stuart Broad, who have by common consensus been England's best players in the series, went on the offensive, hitting as many sixes and fours as they could in a short time in the middle. I don't think the

England team wanted to be here tomorrow any more than we did. Stokes banged a few shots around the place, and I brought Ryan Harris back on for Mitch from the Randwick end. Stokes soon dragged one onto the stumps. Two to go. Board followed a few minutes later, and suddenly – everything has happened so quickly in this match that it almost makes me feel dizzy – we were down to the last pair. It wasn't even drinks time in the last session. We were going to end it by taking seven wickets in less than one hour.

Nobody could have deserved the last wicket more than Ryan Harris. Mitch has been the destroyer since we have been back in Australia, and Sidds has been rock-solid throughout, picking up wickets when we really needed them and bowling in a way that has put on so much pressure that the guy up the other end has dismissed the batsmen, while owing it to Peter. But Ryan Harris – what can I say? He was a bowler of immense potential who could not get on the field for more than three Tests in a row, who missed the first five Test matches we played last year, and then he finally arrived at Lord's. Since then, he has won our man of the series award in England, and would not be far off winning it in Australia. If you put the two series together, it would be impossible to go past Rhino as our most valuable player.

The end all happened so fast. But that's cricket. Rhino flung one down to Boyd Rankin, a bit short of a length, Rankin threw his bat at it and got a thick edge, and before I could think, before I could wonder at how we had got to this point, before I could shed a tear of gratitude for everyone who has put us on the field and stuck with us through some dark times, before I could understand the magnitude of what was happening, my hands were above my eyes and I had the ball in them.

It's over! It's over. Five–nil. We've done it. We've done it!

Wednesday 8 January. Sydney.

The celebrations have been what you would expect after the year we have had, and now I am getting my creaking body ready again for a one-day series, with the first of five matches to be played at the MCG this Sunday. I have been to the gym today, step one, I guess, in putting the Ashes series behind me. That's the thing with cricket: it keeps moving forward and waits for no man. If you spend too long patting yourself on the back for what you have just done, you will be the first man left behind.

I haven't written in my diary for a couple of days. Plenty has happened since then, two nights ago, so I will try to catch up with things.

When we took that final wicket of Boyd Rankin, the boys converged, yelling and screaming, just letting out all that pent-up tension and desire. Once we had shaken the batsmen's hands, Nathan Lyon wanted to capitalise on the emotion of the moment and gathered us on the pitch for a rendition of our song, 'Underneath the Southern Cross I Stand'. I'm not sure if it has ever been done in front of 42,000 spectators before, but it was a highly charged moment for the eleven of us who had been on the field during all five Test matches. I guess Nath knew that later the song would be sung by all of our support staff with us, and this was one just for the eleven players.

We thanked the crowd, nearly all of whom were still in the SCG, and gathered for the official presentation of the Waterford Crystal Ashes trophy and the replica urn. Shane Warne was given presentation duties, and there was a funny moment. As he gave me the crystal trophy, my teammates were starting to climb up onto the stage. Warnie, in his pink McGrath Foundation blazer, knew full well what the boys were liable to do with some bottles of champagne or beer, and quickly made himself scarce before he got saturated. I put the crystal trophy on the side of the stage so it wouldn't get broken. Then Warnie, knowing he still had the tiny replica Ashes urn in his hands, threw it up to me. Fortunately, I caught it. Don't worry. The real thing is under lock and key at Lord's, and the replica, I was later told, was one of those that you can buy in a shop. This one actually belonged to a press photographer. Still, I was glad I didn't drop it!

We had the opportunity to perform a lap of honour, surely one of the biggest pleasures in sport. To go around the ground and see the faces in the crowd who had supported us, and to hear their congratulations and good wishes up close, put a tingle in my spine. There is no discounting the role the Australian crowds have played in this series. Since the Brisbane Test match, and throughout the country, we have felt the strength of their desire power us along like a wave we have ridden. I imagine the English must have felt it too, and they knew that they were not just playing against the eleven Australians on the field.

After my press conference, I hurried back to the changing rooms, where we spent about two hours with family and close friends. The Sydney Cricket Ground home team changing room was as packed as I have ever seen it. This was a special time for the players to thank their loved ones for their help and support, which has been unstinting through the hard times we have gone through.

Our friends and families left as the England team came in, about two hours after the end of the match. I spoke to just about all of the English players, thanking them individually for a good series, and congratulating them on the hard fight they put up. No matter what commentators say or what the final scoreline was, we who were on the field know how tough England were to beat.

I didn't really get a chance to relax. During the two hours or so that the English guys were in our rooms, I had to go out four or five times to fulfil commitments for photographs and television footage. It is a bit like being at your own wedding: you have to go around and make sure everyone is being looked after. Part of my job is to stand up and thank people officially, more than sitting around and chewing the fat as some of the other players from both sides were able to do. I didn't become free to sit down and chat until right at the end of those two hours. I had managed to enjoy some uninterrupted time with our own families and friends, so that was nice.

We stayed in the changing room until just after midnight, before being driven back to the team hotel at the Rocks. A few of us went out with our partners after that. It was a fantastic night, and we enjoyed every minute of our success, reliving all our favourite moments from the last five Test matches. Wherever these eleven players meet in the future, I expect we will be telling stories about the 2013–14 Ashes.

Yesterday, we kept the festivities going with a trip, as a team, to Vaucluse on the harbourfront in Sydney's eastern suburbs, where we were hosted at his home by the businessman Justin Hemmes, a good friend of mine and a big supporter of the Australian team. The team and their partners went, and it was a similar occasion to the one Warnie put on for us in Perth. We were able to enjoy each other's company in private, which is important for the players who spend so much time in the public eye. Everyone loved it. A band played, and our resident musician, Shane Watson, got up with his guitar. A lot of the players remarked on never having seen such a beautiful house and, as a Sydney boy, I was proud to point to the harbour and claim that we were standing before the best view in the world.

Today capped it off, with an official presentation from the Prime Minister, Tony Abbott, on the forecourt of the Sydney Opera House. He said we had been the 'Improbables' for how little chance we had been given to win this series in the way we have, and he said that if we went on to win in South Africa we would then be the new 'Invincibles'. For us, it was terrific to meet thousands more of our fans and say thank you to them. They are loyal Australians who have not taken a step back from their support of us and their belief that we could do it. It was a pleasure to be able to give them something in return. And although the weather had turned a bit cool and drizzly, I still think standing on the shore of Sydney Harbour is the best view in the world. It sure looks good with the Ashes in your hands.

We did it. We returned the urn.

Fifth Test

3–5 January 2014. Sydney Cricket Ground.

Australia (first innings)

Batting		R	B	4	6	SR
CJL Rogers	b: Stokes	11	39	1	0	28.20
DA Warner	b: Broad	16	20	3	0	80.00
SR Watson	lbw: Anderson	43	59	7	0	72.88
MJ Clarke	c: Bell b: Stokes	10	29	1	0	34.48
SPD Smith	c: sub (JE Root) b: Stokes	115	154	17	1	74.67
GJ Bailey	c: Cook b: Broad	1	8	0	0	12.50
BJ Haddin	c: Cook b: Stokes	75	90	13	0	83.33
MG Johnson	c: sub (JE Root) b: Borthwick	12	32	0	0	37.50
RJ Harris	c: Anderson b: Stokes	22	27	2	1	81.48
PM Siddle	c: Bairstow b: Stokes	0	1	0	0	0.00
NM Lyon	not out	1	3	0	0	33.33
Extras	(2lb, 2w, 6nb, 10b)	20				
Total	10 Wkts, 76 overs	326			4.28 Runs/Over	

Fall of wickets 1-22 (Warner, 5.5 ov), 2-51 (Rogers, 15.4 ov), 3-78 (Clarke, 22.3 ov), 4-94 (Watson, 25.4 ov), 5-97 (Bailey, 28.1 ov), 6-225 (Haddin, 55.3 ov), 7-269 (Johnson, 67.3 ov), 8-325 (Harris, 75.1 ov), 9-325 (Siddle, 75.2 ov),10-326 (Smith, 75.6 ov)

Bowling	O	M	R	W	Econ	SR	Extras
JM Anderson	21	3	67	1	3.19	126	
SCJ Broad	19.5	5	65	2	3.27	59.5	(2w)
BA Stokes	19.5	1	99	6	4.99	19.83	(5nb)
WB Rankin	8.2	0	34	0	4.08	–	(1nb)
SG Borthwick	7	0	49	1	7.00	42	

England (first innings)

Batting		R	B	4	6	SR
AN Cook	lbw: Harris	7	19	1	0	36.84
MA Carberry	c: Lyon b: Johnson	0	9	0	0	0.00
JM Anderson	c: Clarke b: Johnson	7	24	1	0	29.16
IR Bell	c: Haddin b: Siddle	2	32	0	0	6.25
KP Pietersen	c: Watson b: Harris	3	9	0	0	33.33
GS Balance	c: Haddin b: Lyon	18	51	2	0	35.29
BA Stokes	b: Siddle	47	101	4	0	46.53
JM Bairstow	c: Bailey b: Siddle	18	50	1	0	36.00
SG Borthwick	c: Smith b: Harris	1	17	0	0	5.88
SCJ Broad	not out	30	22	4	1	136.36
WB Rankin	b: Johnson	13	22	2	0	59.09
Extras	(1lb, 5w, 3nb, 0b)	9				
Total	10 Wkts, 58.5 overs	155			2.63 Runs/Over	

Fall of wickets 1-6 (Carberry, 3.3 ov), 2-8 (Cook, 6.2 ov), 3-14 (Anderson, 9.4 ov), 4-17 (Pietersen, 12.2 ov), 5-23 (Bell, 17.4 ov), 6-62 (Ballance, 31.5 ov), 7-111 (Bairstow, 48.1 ov), 8-112 (Stokes, 48.6 ov), 9-125 (Borthwick, 52.6 ov),10-155 (Rankin, 58.5 ov)

Bowling	O	M	R	W	Econ	SR	Extras
RJ Harris	14	5	36	3	2.57	28	
MG Johnson	13.5	3	33	3	2.38	27.66	(3nb, 5w)
PM Siddle	13	4	23	3	1.76	26	
SR Watson	3	1	5	0	1.66	–	
NM Lyon	15	3	57	1	3.80	90	

Australia (second innings)

Batting		R	B	4	6	SR
CJL Rogers	c & b: Borthwick	119	169	15	0	70.41
DA Warner	lbw: Anderson	16	20	3	0	80.00
SR Watson	c: Bairstow b: Anderson	9	9	2	0	100.00
MJ Clarke	c: Bairstow b: Broad	6	18	1	0	33.33
SPD Smith	c: Cook b: Stokes	7	12	1	0	58.33
GJ Bailey	c: Borthwick b: Broad	46	74	6	0	62.16
BJ Haddin	b: Borthwick	28	40	3	0	70.00
MG Johnson	b: Stokes	4	3	1	0	133.33
RJ Harris	c: Carberry b: Borthwick	13	10	1	1	130.00
PM Siddle	c: Bairstow b: Rankin	4	6	0	0	66.66
NM Lyon	not out	6	10	0	0	60.00
Extras	(14lb, 2w, 2nb, 0b)	18				
Total	10 Wkts, 61.3 overs	276		4.48 Runs/Over		

Fall of wickets 1-27 (Warner, 6.4 ov), 2-47 (Watson, 10.3 ov), 3-72 (Clarke, 15.6 ov), 4-91 (Smith, 20.3 ov), 5-200 (Bailey, 45.4 ov), 6-239 (Haddin, 54.5 ov), 7-244 (Johnson, 55.4 ov), 8-255 (Rogers, 58.2 ov), 9-266 (Harris, 58.6 ov), 10-276 (Siddle, 61.3 ov)

Bowling	O	M	R	W	Econ	SR	Extras
JM Anderson	15	6	46	2	3.06	45	
SCJ Broad	14	1	57	2	4.07	42	(2nb, 1w)
WB Rankin	12.3	0	47	1	3.76	75	
BA Stokes	10	0	62	2	6.20	30	(1w)
SG Borthwick	6	0	33	3	5.50	12	
KP Pietersen	4	1	17	0	4.25	–	

England (second innings)

Batting		R	B	4	6	SR
AN Cook	c: Haddin b: Johnson	7	12	1	0	58.33
MA Carberry	c: Haddin b: Johnson	43	63	8	0	68.25
IR Bell	c: Warner b: Harris	16	19	1	1	84.21
KP Pietersen	c: Bailey b: Harris	6	10	0	0	60.00
GS Balance	lbw Johnson	7	27	1	0	25.92
BA Stokes	c: Bailey b: Lyon	32	16	3	2	200.00
JM Bairstow	c: Clarke b: Lyon	0	3	0	0	0.00
SG Borthwick	c: Clarke b: Lyon	4	2	1	0	200.00
SCJ Broad	b: Harris	42	36	3	4	116.66
JM Anderson	not out	1	1	0	0	100.00
WB Rankin	c: Clarke b: Harris	0	2	0	0	0.00
Extras	(2lb, 0w, 1nb, 5b)	8				
Total	10 Wkts, 31.4 overs	166		5.24 Runs/Over		

Fall of wickets 1-7 (Cook, 1.6 ov), 2-37 (Bell, 9.3 ov), 3-57 (Pietersen, 13.3 ov), 4-87 (Carberry, 21.2 ov), 5-90 (Ballance, 21.5 ov), 6-91 (Bairstow, 22.4 ov), 7-95 (Borthwick, 22.6 ov), 8-139 (Stokes, 29.1 ov), 9-166 (Broad, 31.2 ov), 10-166 (Rankin, 31.4 ov)

Bowling	O	M	R	W	Econ	SR	Extras
RJ Harris	9.4	4	25	5	2.58	11.6	
MG Johnson	9	1	40	3	4.44	18	(1nb)
PM Siddle	4	1	24	0	6.00	–	
NM Lyon	9	0	70	2	7.77	27	

7

Afterword by Kyly Clarke

It is not easy to see your man and his team defeated.

I remember sitting across from Michael at breakfast in Durham the morning after Australia had lost the Fourth Test – and with it the Ashes. I could see the disappointment in his eyes.

Michael HATES losing more than anything and being defeated in England by England, when I knew how much it would have meant to him to win the Ashes as captain . . . well, he was truly gutted.

For a wife in moments like that, it's heartbreaking when you can't do anything to help your husband. You try so hard to put yourself in his shoes, and even when you think you know how he must be feeling, deep down it's nothing compared with the reality. All you can do is keep smiling, help him see the positives and encourage him to keep at it. No one who is great at their game ever gives up.

And one thing I know about my husband Michael is he's a true fighter.

I have never loved a quality in someone as much as I love Michael's determination, passion and dedication to being the absolutely best cricketer and captain he can be for his team and country.

So, leading into the 2013–14 Ashes series in Australia, Michael was still extremely positive. He knew England's 3–0 win in the last series had been much closer than the final score line had shown. In England, and in the months since, he and all the boys had worked hard to improve their game. Michael had faith – a trait you must always hold on to in a game as fickle as cricket.

Unfortunately Michael was struck with another injury in the lead-up. His degenerative back condition – an ailment that has seen him sit on the sidelines more times than he would like – was playing up again and he missed out on the one-day series in India that led into the summer.

Michael lives and breathes cricket and can't wait for the moments he walks onto the field, so not playing was hard on him. Instead, he was visiting his physio to strengthen his back in time for the First Test. A one-hour drive there, an hour's session on the special machine and then another hour getting home, sometimes twice a day . . . that's a lot just to get yourself on the park.

In the days before the First Test in Brisbane, Michael was very nervous but at the same time excited for what was to come. Positivity breeds success and Michael was training the house down every day. For weeks I kept hearing him say: 'If we win the First Test, babe, we'll win the Ashes!!!'

He mentioned there was a certain part of his game he had to work on because that's where England was going to attack him. And he was right! In the first innings he got out the exact way he knew England was going to bowl to him.

That was tough to swallow for Michael. It's never easy for him to brush off the expectations he puts on himself. But experience has taught him the knack of putting aside personal performance to focus on the issue at hand: winning for the team. Fortunately his second-innings century did just that!

Arriving a couple of days before the Second Test in Adelaide, Michael and I got some quality time together for lunch and shopping where we stumbled across some lucky charms. I have always been a spiritual person, so I gifted Michael an 'evil eye' charm, and he gifted me the same in a bracelet. I vowed to wear it the whole summer in the hope it would rid Michael and the team of bad vibes. In fact, I took the superstition one step further during the Adelaide Test, sitting in the same 'lucky' seat and never getting up unless it was a drinks break. Sure enough, Michael scored another century and Australia won again to go 2–0 up!

The Third Test in Perth was a memorable one, with most of the family there for Michael's hundredth Test. Michael is not big on statistics – I think we as his family were prouder than he was for this milestone – but for this great moment I gave Michael a handwritten leather book of his top 100 moments in cricket. I wanted him to remember all the great achievements along the way. I was cheeky enough to leave a couple of spots open at the end, because I knew he had more amazing innings to come.

Perth was where the Australian cricket team finally achieved their mission to 'return the urn'!

All us wives and girlfriends cheered and I embraced Michael's father, Les, congratulating him and thanking God that it all went our way. None of us could've been happier. My hands were sore from clapping so hard. I had tears in my eyes – tears of joy and excitement for my man, along with tears of relief. It wasn't my Ashes to win, but a weight had been lifted off my shoulders too.

After the presentations the boys walked past the crowd to the change rooms and Michael saw me. To my surprise, and with such confidence, he stepped over the railing, walked straight up and gave me the world's biggest kiss. 'Thank you,' he whispered. 'I love you and I couldn't do it without you'. I'll never forget that feeling of recognition and appreciation – all the little things I'd tried to do to help Michael along the way had paid off! I smiled from ear to ear as I wiped tears from my eyes.

That legend Warnie threw a party at the luxurious Crown Metropol Mansion Apartments where he was staying. Waiters served drinks and food all night long and Chris Rogers and Doug Bollinger burned up the dance floor. It was the best party we have had with the team to date, but my favourite part was hubby and I eating toasted cheese and ham sandwiches in the pool in the early hours of the morning. It always seems to be the smallest things that make you smile most.

There's no rest for the wicket! Home in Sydney, we celebrated our family Christmas early as usual with beautiful food and wonderful company. All the ladies of our collective clans cooked their favourite dish for a table full of homemade specials and Michael tried his hand at being Santa by handing out our Kris Kringle gifts but lasted five minutes, having no idea of the concept (luckily I buy the gifts for both of us!).

Late on Christmas afternoon, after the Cricket Australia lunch, we decided to crash the Warne family Christmas. It was a gorgeous summer's day, with bombs in the pool, some sunbaking and pool played by the boys. My favourite part of the celebration was the smile on Michael's face. He was calm, relaxed, content – a happy soul. Santa had already come for Michael – the Ashes was his perfect Christmas present.

New Year's Eve with the team was spent at our team hotel. We enjoyed the 9.00 pm fireworks, then turned in. I watched the Harbour Bridge light up the skies while hubby slept through it. A midnight kiss on the forehead and a whisper of 'May God gift you a whitewash this year' and I was lights out.

With the Ashes in the bag – well, in the urn actually – Michael was relaxed. But there's something he always says before EVERY Test . . . and the week before the Fifth Test in Sydney was no different. He'll be thinking about the batting line-up and then he'll look over to me. Before he even opens his mouth, I say: 'Don't tell me, you want a hundred this Test, right, babe?' followed by a little giggle.

I can't describe the feeling of finally seeing Michael hold up the Ashes urn in victory. It's amazing that something so small can mean so very much and it truly does for all of us. To see my husband accomplish one of the biggest achievements in cricket brought tears to my eyes. Along with some of the other partners, I celebrated their win at the SCG and then again in front of the public at a reception at the Opera House with the harbour in the background! You couldn't have written a better script and the smile on Michael's face for weeks afterward could have lit up a room.

Cheers to a wonderful few months of cricket, congratulations to a team with such determination, thank you to the support staff for always backing our boys and to the wives, girlfriends and families that allow us to have the best team representing our country!

Salute,
Kyly Clarke x

8

CONCLUSIONS

This has been my second diary to cover these back-to-back Ashes series in England and Australia. All I can say is, what a difference a year makes! To go away and lose a series 0–3, and follow it up by winning 5–0, is a turnaround that has not been seen very often in the history of cricket. We followed it up by defeating England 4–1 in the one-day international series and 3–0 in the Twenty20 series. And then we went to South Africa and defeated the world's number one team 2–1 in a Test series in their own backyard. Almost a year since we finished our disastrous tour of India, we were achieving our goal of displacing South Africa at the top of the ICC Test rankings.

What everyone wants to know is: How did we achieve such a reversal? I am not sure if I have an answer that will satisfy everyone, but from my vantage point as

Australian captain, I will do my best. But bear in mind that sport is not an exact science. If you knew precisely why you achieved an outcome, you could repeat it at will. There is too much uncertainty in sport for me to say that I have all the answers. And nor would I want to. I am as ambitious and zealous now about improving myself as a cricketer as I ever was. Our goals still lie ahead of us, and if we want to achieve them we have to keep getting better. If we thought we knew all the answers, there is no way we would get to the top.

In the following pages, I will outline some of the themes in our team play that have developed through the past year. I hope they give some indication of why we were able to achieve such an amazing turnaround.

Planning and preparation

When I wrote *The Ashes Diary* about our 2013 tour of England, I might have surprised a lot of people by how upbeat I was about our performance there and about our chances of turning the result around in Australia. We had just lost our third Ashes series in a row, and it was the first time in many years that Australia had lost a series to England without winning a Test match. Three–nil is pretty definitive.

And yet, I was writing about how the mood in our team was very strong. Even from the outside, observers

244

were saying how unusual it was for a team to go through a 0–3 series result away from home and end up looking stronger at the end than they had at the beginning. Normally things unravel when results don't go your way on the road. We didn't. In defeat, we grew tougher and hungrier and more united.

I always had confidence in the boys, and the boys had confidence in each other. We knew something about ourselves that probably wasn't apparent to the outside world, who hadn't seen all the hard work we were putting in behind the scenes.

This work consists of planning and preparing as much as practising cricket skills. You can't just go out and practise on automatic pilot, as if everything will take care of itself. Practice has to be targeted at strengthening your weaknesses, improving on your strengths, and perfecting the plans you have developed for your opposition.

Our tour of England was a time in which we built and refined our plans. For some batsmen, such as Alastair Cook, we settled on our bowling plans quite early and pursued them throughout the ten Test matches. It was a matter of having the discipline and control to execute the lines and lengths we wanted to bowl. For other batsmen, such as Ian Bell, who did so well against us in England, we had to revise and create new plans once we were back in Australia. We bowled quite differently to him in the five Test matches in Australia, and the results were there to see. For all the English batsmen, from one to eleven, we talked about our plans, took feedback from the bowlers and fielders, and got ourselves to the point where the bowlers knew precisely what they wanted to do when they got the ball in their hands.

Putting the ball in the right place is a big part of the puzzle, but not the only part. Another element is having the field settings that will complement the bowling. It was widely remarked upon, and noticed by everyone, that I was prepared to depart from the textbook in some of my field placings. On slow wickets, to a batsman such as Kevin Pietersen who loves playing on the front foot, I would deploy several catchers in unorthodox positions in the arc between square leg and mid-on. When the wicket was bouncier, I tried leg slips in a number of placements and a short leg behind, rather than in front of, square. There are thousands of places on a cricket field where you can put a man. The textbook shouldn't be an unbreakable prescription. In devising all these placements, I drew on all the knowledge I had around me, whether that was in our bowlers and fielders, in our coaching staff, or outside the group in the voices of former Australian players. I am pragmatic and results-focused, and I don't particularly care how we get there. So when it comes to gathering information and developing bowling plans, my one rule is, there are no rules.

Similarly, in how we used our bowlers there was no guide except the needs of the present moment. There is nothing to say the right length of a spell for a bowler is five overs, six overs, seven overs or one over. I follow my instincts. It was noticed that Mitch Johnson bowled in short spells, usually three or four overs at a time, but that wasn't a preordained plan. Sometimes I only gave him two overs. I just changed the bowling when it felt right.

So I guess what I'm saying is, a captain has to strike a balance between planning and letting go of the plan. But one thing is for sure: if you don't have good plans in the first place, you don't have the option of changing them. You can only improvise if you have a script to play from.

The improvement in our batting over the course of the year was also a result of planning and preparation. At the beginning of our tour of England, I said we had to concentrate on tightening our defence as a go-to for when conditions were difficult and we were under pressure. We had been losing wickets in clumps too often in India, and continued to do so at times in England. Our response was to work on our defensive plans, and for each of us, as individuals, to develop a plan to counter each English bowler.

This did not mean we were changing our batting philosophy to become more defensive. Far from it. You can't tell David Warner to bat like Chris Rogers (or vice versa); there is no surer way to wreck a player's game than to direct him to take it away from what feels natural. But unless we had a good defence to fall back on in times of trouble, we could not respond to different circumstances. You can't hit your way out of every situation. And I think ultimately this paid off. We played some very positive, attacking cricket, but if you go back and look closely at the many fine innings played by David Warner, Chris Rogers, Shane Watson, Steve Smith, George Bailey and Brad Haddin, even though many were characterised by memorable attacking shots, there was a strong current of solid defence running underneath them. Davey and Hadds were our top scorers in the home series, and their aggression was rightly praised. But it can't be forgotten that they batted in Test cricket style, with a lot of leaving the ball, defending good balls, and remaining water-tight in defence. Without that go-to, there is no possibility of branching out into the attacking side of the game. Whenever I saw one of those guys play a great innings, I was clapping like anyone else for the flashing boundaries and exciting strokeplay. But what I also saw was how much work those guys had put in at practice, in the nets with the bowlers and the coaches, in planning meetings, and in their own personal preparation. What you saw on the field was only the end result of a long process.

The support staff

Our support staff, led by coach Darren Lehmann and manager Gavin Dovey, left no stone unturned in their preparation for every detail of the Ashes series, on and off the field. Darren brought a fresh attitude to the job when he took it on in England, and deserves all the credit he has been given. He was one of many who worked for us behind the scenes. I have no doubt that ours is the best support staff in world cricket.

On the cricket side of things, we had experienced former players doing the coaching, such as our batting coach Mike di Venuto, our bowling coach Craig McDermott, and our fielding coaches Steve Rixon and Mike Young. Dene Hills, the former Tasmanian opening batsman, was our keen-eyed analyst who provided a wealth of useful information. But that is not to forget people like Peter Brukner, who looked after us as our doctor; Alex Kountouris, with whom I spent more time than just about anyone else; Damien Mednis, who got our strength and conditioning just right; and many other people in different roles, both with the team and at Cricket Australia, all working towards the same end, which is the success of Australian cricket. I think that is going to be the really memorable feature of this summer: how everyone was working as a united team.

Hunger

If there was one upside of losing three Ashes series in a row since 2009, and losing the last one 0–3, it was that we were totally sick of losing, and we refused to tolerate it anymore. I think this is one of the great strengths of

Australian cricket. We *hate* losing. We have had so much success in the past, we will not put up with an extended run of defeat. We have a winning culture. We watched England celebrate at Trent Bridge when they beat us so narrowly, at Lord's when they thrashed us, and when they retained the Ashes at Old Trafford. We watched them enjoy their win at Chester-le-Street. We stood and watched them celebrate when they received the urn at The Oval. It hurt like hell every time. But this is not a hurt that you can avoid. If you avoid it, you can't use it as fuel. And every member of this team fuelled himself with the pain of that experience.

I saw evidence of that hunger in our attitude to practice and to meetings, and I saw it on the field. I can't say we were more hungry than England by the time the Brisbane Test match rolled around, because I was not in the England changing room. But what I can say is that there was a desire in the Australian team that would not be quenched. It was still there on the last afternoon in Brisbane, when we didn't go overboard celebrating the win, because we knew we hadn't won anything yet. I saw that desire in Adelaide, when the boys went out and played a relentless, grinding brand of cricket on a surface that did us no favours. I saw the desire in the heat in Perth, where we held our nerve when the Ashes came within our reach.

Often in cricket, when the achievement is attained, the hunger goes away. But so strong was the hunger in our team, once we had won the Ashes in Perth we just wanted more. That is a measure of how sick of losing we had become. That is how much fuel was in our tanks after losing in England. So when we went to Melbourne and Sydney, we had as much desire to play our brand of cricket and win those matches as we had had in Brisbane. I didn't detect any less intensity in the Fifth Test match than I had seen in the First.

Aggressive cricket

When we talk of our 'brand' of cricket, what we mean is that we would like to play as if we are not afraid to lose. This is easier said than done, and in a way it puts professional sport in a nutshell. Of course you don't want to lose, but if you let it become a fear, it can paralyse you. You must somehow find a way to be bold and brave, and play without fear. Throughout the Ashes series, you could see this probably nowhere more visibly than when Brad Haddin went out to bat. Aside from in Adelaide, in the first innings of each Test match we had fewer than 200 runs on the board when Hadds went out there. Of course he hated the very idea of losing, but he did not let it inhibit him. Instead, he looked as free as if he was having a practice hit. Not only did he get us out of trouble, but he was truly inspirational to the changing room in the *way* he did it. There was no digging in for survival, no time-wasting, no seeking excuses. He just went out there and counter-attacked. He managed to free his mind so that, no matter what pressure he was under, he batted as if he was in his local park on a Saturday afternoon.

That's just one example – though Hadds did it in every Test match – of an attitude that permeated the whole team. Whenever I gave Peter Siddle the ball, even if his task was to slow the scoring rate, he did it in a positive, aggressive way. Whenever Chris Rogers or David Warner left the new ball to pass outside their off stump, they counted it as a small victory over the bowler. You can play a positive, aggressive 'leave' as much as a positive, aggressive straight drive past the bowler.

We saw this positive intent grow in Nathan Lyon throughout the series. His job is not to be the new Shane Warne, it is to be the new Nathan Lyon. If he had been tentative in the way he went about tying down the English batsmen, he wouldn't have taken so many key wickets. But he believed in himself, and very soon the English batsmen had to respect him as the dangerous bowler he became.

In the field, we never let up on our First Test mantra of 'Every run counts'. We fielded in a way that showed we enjoyed every moment of the great privilege of playing Test cricket. As a consequence, our misfields were few and our catching was almost faultless. There were some great catches, such as David Warner's match-changing effort to dismiss Michael Carberry in the first innings in Adelaide, Mitch Johnson's catch of Kevin Pietersen at mid-on in the first innings in Perth, Ryan Harris's of the same batsman at long-on in the second, and several of George Bailey's close-in grabs, but what is even more pleasing is how few authentic chances we put down. Fielding and catching are the barometers of a cricket team's mindset, and our fielders were always making our bowlers feel that they were being supported. At the same time, they were making the English batsmen feel that they were surrounded, in a state of siege.

The verbal side of cricket is part of the aggression of the game. I was going to say 'modern' game, but it has always been a part of cricket. The Australian team sometimes cops a bit of flak for its verbal aggression, but we make no apologies when we stay within the code of conduct, and these days there is not much difference, on the verbal side, between all international teams.

As I have said before, though, the verbal part of the game is not designed to hurt the opponent. It is about getting ourselves up for the battle. Some of us need it at times, while some of us do not. It is up to the individual to get the best out of himself. It is the same with players on the opposing team. On occasion it does go overboard, and I put my hand up to apologise for swearing at James Anderson in the dying stages of the Brisbane Test match. Later, when we went to South Africa, I also said some things in the heat of the moment to Dale Steyn in the Third Test match at Cape Town that I later apologised for. We're not perfect – far from it. But I can say that I am proud of the positive energy that has emanated from the Australian team all summer, both at home and in South Africa.

Fast bowling

Cricket fans love fast bowling. It has always been the way. Australian fans who had been brought up on Dennis Lillee and Jeff Thomson also loved watching the great West Indian fast bowlers, even when they were giving our boys a touch-up. In Craig McDermott and Merv Hughes, we had two inspirational fast bowlers when I was watching the Australian team as a kid. There can be few more exciting sights than seeing a top-class fast bowler roaring in and bowling accurately, whether short or full of a length, testing out the batsmen's full range of skills.

Mitchell Johnson brought this great tradition of fast bowling back to the forefront of our cricket in the 2013–14 Ashes series. Mitch was man of the match in three of the five Test matches, and man of the series. But the wickets he took don't tell you about the mood he created. In Brisbane, he was truly awesome to watch. Before the series, when we knew he was bowling so fast, we developed a new set of plans to deal with England's tail-end batsmen. Tail-enders can dictate the course of a match and a series. At Lord's, Graeme Swann,

Tim Bresnan and Stuart Broad scored vital runs. Broad's batting at Trent Bridge proved the difference between us winning and losing. At Durham, it was Bresnan again scoring runs that turned out to be decisive in the context of that Test match. And we all have bad memories of Monty Panesar and James Anderson holding us off at Cardiff in 2009. So you can't leave tail-end batsmen out of your plans. We had a clear design for Mitchell to bowl short and give the English tail a hard time. From Brisbane onwards, we saw the results. None of those guys was a factor with the bat in this series.

Against the top-order batsmen, Mitch was complemented beautifully in the pace department by Ryan Harris, Peter Siddle and Shane Watson. Rhino's pace was often close to Mitch's and I will remember the ball he dismissed Alastair Cook with in the second innings in Perth for as long as I live. Fielding in slips to such bowling is an exciting cricket experience; you live for that feeling.

After the series, Kevin Pietersen said that people watching the game can't guess how much harder it is facing accurate bowling at 150 kilometres per hour compared with 140. He was right, as we found when facing Morne Morkel and Dale Steyn in South Africa. Morkel, in particular, targeted us with some very fast short-pitched bowling. After Mitch dominated the First Test match at Centurion, Morne began to give us a dose of our own medicine in Port Elizabeth. Dale followed it up with some peerless reverse-swing bowling in the second innings. Express fast bowling was the critical factor in both of those matches, for us first and then for South Africa. Finally, in the deciding Test match in Cape Town, Morne went after me in the first innings with a pretty sustained short-pitched attack. He hit me on the arm, in the neck, on the shoulder, on the finger, and a few other places as well. I won't pretend that I loved it, but I do have a full first-hand appreciation of how nightmarish it can be to face express bowling. You sure know you have been in a battle. And when you get on top of it, as we managed to do in Cape Town, victory tastes sweet indeed.

Our improved batting

In the Ashes series, our top order consistency was by no means perfect. Only in Adelaide did we post a big first-innings score. But it was a series in which every batsman managed to chip in when needed. Davey Warner got big scores in the second innings in Brisbane, Adelaide and Perth. Chris Rogers made hundreds on the two worst batting wickets of the series, in Melbourne and Sydney. Shane Watson destroyed the English bowling in Perth and, alongside Chris, made a tough chase look comfortable in Melbourne. Steve Smith confirmed his rise as a Test-class batsman with hundreds in the first innings in Perth and Sydney. George Bailey always batted with the team's needs at the top of his mind, notched a debut Test half-century in Adelaide, and broke a world record in Perth. Hadds made a half-century or a century in the first innings of every match. I chipped in in Brisbane and Adelaide, and although I would have liked to have made more runs in the back half of the series, the best thing for me personally was to feel less central to our batting. Opposition teams a couple of years ago might have looked at our results and said that Australia only made big scores when I did. They can't say that anymore, and that is a triumph for our batting unit and our support staff.

Things only got better for our batting group in South Africa. In the First Test match at Centurion, David Warner, Alex Doolan, Shaun Marsh and Steve Smith all made significant contributions. To see a group of young batsmen prospering on a really difficult wicket against Steyn, Morkel and Vernon Philander was a huge thrill. Shaun's first-innings hundred, in his return match for Australia after a two-year absence, was one of the best innings you could hope to see, and he probably would have been man of the match if not for Mitch Johnson's sublime bowling. In the Second Test match at Port Elizabeth, our first innings batting let us down, but in the second innings Chris Rogers scored a century for the ages, on a truly fiendish deteriorating wicket. In the decider, I got into the runs at last but Davey overshadowed everyone with two magnificent hundreds. He batted well in every Test match in South Africa and was a most deserving man of the series. As a unit, we could stand up and say, over the course of the three Test matches, that we didn't need Hadds and the bowlers to dig us out of trouble.

How did we come so far since the dark days in India and England in 2013? I think that one reason is that we have to face the best bowling attack in the world on a daily basis, in the nets. When you have got Ryan Harris, Mitchell Johnson, Shane Watson and Peter Siddle steaming in at you, with Nathan Lyon probing away for any weakness against spin, you know you have to be batting well. You get a rest from them only to have the likes of James Faulkner, James Pattinson, Jackson Bird and Nathan Coulter-Nile coming at you. It is not comfortable. Then, in the spin department, you have to face Nathan Lyon. There is no rest at all. So I think one big reason for our improved batting was the quality of our practice.

What I was most proud of in the improvement of our batting was that each player developed, and followed, his own way. David Warner certainly doesn't bat like Chris Rogers, but neither opener felt like he had to imitate the other. When Bucky was struggling, he didn't try to hit his way out of trouble. When Davey was not scoring as freely as he liked, he didn't decide to entrench himself. Each opener followed his own lights. Shane Watson played his own way, as did everyone in the middle order. Brad Haddin certainly played his own way, and we all reaped the benefits. I think that when teams play us now, they see a batting unit that knows its own mind and trusts in the Australian way.

Experience

This applies across the board, but I can easily start with batting. When we lost those matches in India and England last year, a lot of our batsmen were still coming to terms with the demands of Test cricket. Players like David Warner and Steve Smith still had only a handful of Test matches under their belt when they went to India. Everyone gets better with experience, if they learn from it, and this is one way of telling our story: we are a much more seasoned group of players now than we were a year ago. There is no substitute for those 17 Test matches we have played since the start of the tour of India. A lot of it was ugly experience, but you don't learn as much about yourself in cricket when things are all going your way.

Likewise, the bowlers have gained experience. Nathan Lyon, who started this period as a bowler still getting used to the Test arena, has transformed himself into a match-hardened spin bowler, having gone through all the ups and downs that are part of the spinner's lot. Ryan Harris, although he came into Test cricket at a mature age, still had relatively little Test experience before the tour of England. Peter Siddle became a fixture in our team and played his 50th Test match in Melbourne, as did Shane Watson. If I look around our changing room now, I see guys I have fought alongside for a long time. That is an immense comfort. We trust each other, because we know we can prevail together.

This year has been a real coming-of-age for three of those players in particular. David Warner, Steve Smith and Nathan Lyon have made the journey from inexperienced Test cricketers in their mid-20s to mainstays of the Australian team for now and, I hope, a long time to come. As a senior player, that feels wonderful.

As painful as losing was, you don't gain experience without it. The lows we suffered in India and England were essential to the hunger we brought home to Australia. And there are specific aspects to this, that we learned to use for our benefit. For instance, at Chester-le-Street, when Stuart Broad got on a roll and proved too much for us to handle, we learned a lot about momentum. When we had the opportunity to turn the tables, we applied that lesson. We might not have been able to put that momentum to its best effect in Australia if we hadn't undergone that horrible experience in England. So in a way, we can thank the English team for being our teachers during that painful time.

Continuity

It's a chicken-and-egg argument, in a way. You like to maintain consistency and continuity in selection, because players gain a sense of security and are not continually worried about their places. How can they play without fear of losing a game when they are worried about losing their place in the team? But you can only have that continuity if you are achieving success on the field. And the success sometimes doesn't come unless the continuity is there in the first place. So what comes first, the continuity or the results?

During the Ashes series at home, we played with the same eleven cricketers for the first time ever in a five-match series. It was an amazing achievement and knitted us together with a fantastic spirit of unity. But that is not to say that in England, when we used 17 players, the selectors were doing the wrong thing. They were trying to find a combination, and eventually they found it. The outcome is that you feel fantastic to be standing up on the Sydney Cricket Ground at the beginning of the fifth Test match of the summer, linking arms with the same ten guys you have been with throughout the series. When you know that your opponent is shuffling through the deck with new selections, it makes you feel even more unified. It is a bond that the eleven of us will share forever.

Team first

All this adds up to a feeling that can't be beaten. Cricket is a unique sport, in that it places individual battles, for batsmen and bowlers and wicketkeepers and fielders, within the context of a team game. Separating the team goals from the individual goals is a challenge to every cricketer. It is only human for guys who have scored a hundred runs or taken five wickets to feel contented with themselves in a losing changing room. And conversely, it would only be human for guys who have had a lean Test match personally to feel a bit unsatisfied even when their team has won. This is a facet of cricket at every level.

But I have rarely played in any team that put the group above the individual as much as the Australian Test team of the past year. No gimmicks, no 'bonding' exercises, no buzz-words were necessary: we all put our team first. You could see that in the way someone like George Bailey would go out and bat, with his career on the line, and instead of preserving his own wicket he'd try to score quick runs for his team. You could see it in how readily Mitchell Johnson accepted my decision to bowl him in short spells. You could see it in how unhesitatingly David Warner accepted my decision to declare in Adelaide when he was only 17 runs from a Test match century. 'Whatever's best for the team.' I could name every player and give examples of where he put the team's interests above his own statistics. And it carried through to the way we looked after each other as well. The times I got a bit over-heated in the on-field verbal side of things were where I was stepping up to look after a junior teammate, whether it was George Bailey in Brisbane or James Pattinson in Cape Town, when I confronted Steyn. I don't think I necessarily did these things in the best way, but the theme is what I want to illustrate: it was all about Australian players standing up for each other.

You could see it even in the last act of the summer. In Cape Town, we had a day and a half to dismiss South Africa in the fourth innings and win the series. It was very hard, because they have a world-class batting line-up who are not only superb attacking players when they need to be, but also world-class defenders. We had seen this in Adelaide last year, when they defied us for a similar length of time. In Cape Town, again it was guys like AB de Villiers and Faf du Plessis who blocked and blocked for hours, attritional batting of the highest calibre. It was hellish to go through, to be honest. And in the last session of the last day, they were still holding out. Dale Steyn and Vernon Philander were proving impossible to budge. Our bowlers were absolutely exhausted. They were spent. We were very frustrated at the thought of getting this close and falling short. The crowd were heckling me for declaring too late. I was doubting myself. At the end, with five overs to go, I had to turn to our aces, Mitchell Johnson and Ryan Harris. But they were gone, they were finished. Mitch had bowled with a sustained fury for months, and he had nothing left to give. Ryan had nagged and nagged until his right knee was just a mess of bits of bone and cartilage. I went to him and asked if he could bowl.

He could barely walk, let alone bowl! He said, 'If I can't bowl, who will?' I looked around. Everyone was buggered. I said, 'If you don't bowl, I will.' Ryan looked at me and shook his head. 'Okay,' he said. There was no way he was going to leave it to me – and rightly so. That's what I call putting the team first. With a yorker he bowled Steyn, and with a beautiful late in-dipper from around the wicket, he clipped Morne Morkel's off stump. We had beaten South Africa, because Australian cricketers had put their team first.

World number one

A few weeks after we came home from South Africa, the news came through: under the International Cricket Council's rankings system, we were now number one in the world in both Test and one-day cricket.

I don't think I've had a more satisfied feeling in my whole career.

Just 12 months earlier, when I stated that my goal was for us to be number one in all three forms of the game (including Twenty20, which I no longer play), there would not have been too many people who shared my belief. Maybe some of them were saying I was kidding myself. We had just come back from India, where we were beaten 4–0 in the Test series. We were about to fall at the first hurdle in the one-day Champions' Trophy in

England, and would then lose our first two Ashes Test matches on the way to our third straight series defeat against England. Yet I still believed we could be number one in the world, and I was still saying so, both in public and to the team in private.

Who believed me?

Some of the people who had seen the way we played in India might even have been laughing at me. We were called the worst Australian team ever to tour India. It's the last thing you want to hear. We had slumped so far that we were ranked the number five Test nation in the world. I think back to the last day of the Second Test match of the 2013 Ashes series, at Lord's, where I was interviewed on the field after our loss. When I said I thought we could come back from there and win the series 3–2, people in the crowd – quite a lot of people in the crowd – did laugh at me. It wasn't a good feeling. Then I went into a press conference where I was told that Kim Hughes was the last Australian Test captain to lose six matches in a row, as I had just done, and it had led to his resignation. Was that where I was headed? By then, I had to allow for every possibility.

It breaks your heart, to be honest. Not because of what I had to go through personally as the team's public face. I could cope with that. What really upset me was that I knew how hard the players in our changing room were working, and how they must have felt that they had nothing to show for it. They were gutted. We were not an experienced Test cricket team, but we were endeavouring with every fibre in our bodies to get better at this game each day. We held ourselves to high standards. We pulled together. But we had just lost six straight Test matches, and there is only so long you can keep going without the reassurance and the nourishment that winning can give you. Darren Lehmann hit the nail on the head at his first press conference when, in tumultuous circumstances at the start of that tour, he became our head coach. What, he was asked, was his chief aim with this team? He replied with one word: 'Winning.'

But in the weeks since he had started in the job, we were two losses from two Test matches. That was what had me worried: how much longer could we keep up with our professionalism and our team ideals if we didn't have some on-field success to show for it?

Things did turn around during that series, if slowly. In Manchester, we dominated the Test match and had England on the ropes before the rain closed in and washed out most of the last day. We needed that win so much. We knew we had the upper hand. But would we have won the match if it hadn't rained? We didn't know. We still had seven wickets to take. It's cricket; anything could have happened. We thought we could win, but we would be fools if we mentally chalked that match up in our column.

Then, at Durham and the Oval, we had the better of England for substantial periods of both Test matches.

But we didn't close out the wins. England built up great momentum on the last day in Durham, and stole a match that we considered we were in a position to win. All of our good work ended up counting for nothing. At the Oval, where it rained for almost two days, I did my best to engineer a situation from which we could take a win – but we also might have come away with another defeat. We couldn't pretend that was a moral victory either. There is no such thing.

At the end of that tour, Boof said that we could have won the series 3–2. He was right. Stuart Broad said England could have won it 5–0. He was also right. But either way, I wasn't prepared to deal in the might-have-beens. I only looked at the scoresheets, and they said we had lost the series 3–0. We were a long, long way from number one.

This team has been through so much together, and the taste of success is so much sweeter for what we suffered for most of 2013. It was a long, long year.

One of the things about that period that really hurt me was that I was the only player left in the team who had had a taste of extended success, and I wanted the others to share it. When I came into the Australian cricket team, not only were we number one, but we had been in that position for the best part of a decade. We had won two one-day World Cups, and were on our way to winning a third on the trot. We had a lot of great players, and being the best in the world was something that was expected, both from within and outside the team. They were great days, and I was so lucky to be part of it.

The guys I play with now had not tasted that kind of success for themselves. This was another thing that made me really sorry on their behalf. They deserved it every bit as much as the great team I had entered, but they weren't getting it. Many people outside the team were willing to just accept passively that the wheel had turned. The great players such as Shane Warne, Glenn McGrath, Adam Gilchrist and Justin Langer, and many others, had retired within a couple of years of each other, and Australian cricket had to face the fact that we had enjoyed a long time at the top and now it was someone else's turn.

I never saw Ricky Ponting accept the 'turn of the wheel' as if it was inevitable, and as a fellow survivor of those great teams I never accepted it either. Sure, South Africa, England and India developed strong records of success and gave us a touch-up from time to time. But there is no rule that says that when great players retire, the team's run of success has to come to an end. Of course, it can happen. We have seen it with the West Indies. But we had cricketers coming into our team who were talented enough to take us back to the top. We had a fantastic coaching staff and support from Cricket Australia and most of the Australian public. Yes, we did struggle at times after 2008, but there was no ironclad rule that said it had to keep on that way.

When you want to win so much but you haven't done it yet, one of the hardest things to generate is self-belief. It can take a long time, and it goes through many trials and tests, both at the individual level and in the team. Did Mitchell Johnson believe he was the most damaging fast bowler in the world, and someone who would terrify opposition batsmen? Over the years, he had shown glimpses of that, but it wasn't until late 2013, when he came back into the Australian team, that he knew it for sure. Did Ryan Harris know that he was one of the best fast bowlers in cricket today? He might have sensed that he had that potential, but due to injuries and a late start at the international level, he hadn't really proven that until this year. I could go through all of our team and describe a similar journey. Even someone like David Warner, who lacks absolutely nothing in the self-belief department, could not know for sure that he was at the top rung of international batsmen until he had the results to prove it. As for myself, it doesn't matter how many runs I have scored in the past, I always feel nervous when I go out to bat, and I always wonder if I am going to be good enough today. All cricketers, when you peel away the outer skin, have experienced self-doubt, no matter what their record. I value Shane Warne's counsel so much in part because he helps to build up my self-belief as a batsman. Self-doubt affects us all. So when we are looking to build up our confidence, it is a complex formula with lots of different factors involved.

But there's no question that being able to look at your record and see that you have won games in the past is a prime ingredient in having the belief that you are going to win games in the future.

As a team, did we know we had it in us to be number one again? When we beat England in Brisbane in November, I could sense a real breakthrough. Now we had something to show for all our hard work. But still, cricket is cricket. Adelaide was going to be a hard match for us to win on a wicket that would suit England's style of play. We competed fantastically well there, and it would have been a travesty if we hadn't come away with a win. The forecast rain held off, and we got the win fairly comfortably. The team's belief in itself went up another notch.

Then, in Perth, we found an England team that was really prepared to dig in for its last stand to save the Ashes. That was a hard, hard match. We had some nervous moments in the fourth innings, but we got there. Our celebrations were full of joy and relief, but we knew we weren't finished. Success is so sweet and failure is so bitter. Now that we were in this situation, there was no way in the world we wanted to go back to where we had been. We had this fantastic experience of winning, but the memory of defeat was so real, and so recent, that it drove us on.

In Melbourne, we didn't play at our best for a lot of the Test match, but we came through when the game was on the line. That was a different way of winning, and extremely satisfying for that reason. We could win games from in front, and now we could win them from behind. Our self-belief went up another notch. By Sydney, we were a bit like a runaway train, and we made the momentum we had built up count for everything, by not letting England have so much as a sniff.

The break after the Ashes series posed another challenge. We did well in the home one-day series, but to go to South Africa and play the world number one team on their turf – well, there were a lot of doubters again saying that the England team we had beaten were not so good, and we would get our come-uppance against the likes of Smith, Steyn, Morkel, Amla and de Villiers on their home wickets.

The spirit we had going to South Africa was very different from what we had taken into the Ashes series at home. In November, we thought we were better than our results showed, but we still didn't know it for certain. By February, we had the proof. The self-belief was there. But this is cricket, and every day is a new one. Every match, you start with no runs and no wickets. If things had turned around in our favour so quickly against England, what was to say that they couldn't turn against us again just as fast? South Africa hadn't been beaten at home for five years. They deserved to be world number one. But we knew – not just hoped, but knew – that we were good enough to beat them if we played at our best.

What we went there and produced, everyone who saw it will remember for their whole lives. This was a great series of cricket of the highest calibre. We won so well in Centurion that we confirmed we had brought our confidence from Australia with us. But then, South Africa hit back in Port Elizabeth so hard that all of a sudden we were the underdogs again. In the decider in Cape Town, we had a fantastic first day with the bat, and got ahead in the match. Still, by day five, South Africa fought so tenaciously that we needed every ounce of energy and self-belief to finally get the result we craved. It was the most amazing feeling to achieve that, and I'll never forget the sense of satisfaction.

And it was that win that got us the world number one ranking. By the time this diary is published, a wrinkle in the ICC's rankings system will mean that South Africa are number one again. So be it. It's not a bad thing, as it will remind us that we can take nothing for granted. We have to start from the base again and climb that mountain. It has to be done again, versus a very dangerous Pakistan team in the Emirates, and then versus the confident Indians in Australia. It will have to be done against every team we face. Now that we are number one, our opponents will be working all the harder to knock us off. We have a target on our backs.

The South African series felt, and ultimately was, a play-off for the number one ranking, a kind of unofficial world championship of cricket. If number one is a 'title', we won it in the only fitting way, by going to the reigning number one's backyard and beating them there. In one-day cricket, we also have to back up our ranking with titles. In the last World Cup and the last Champions' Trophy, we didn't progress to the final rounds. We may be number one based on our consistency over the years, but we are not World Champions. That task lies ahead of us in Australia and New Zealand in 2015. As I said at the beginning of 2013, I had three immediate aims as captain: to win the Ashes, to be ranked world number one, and to win the 2015 World Cup. While the waves of unrest and defeat were rocking us, those three aims were out there on the horizon that I was trying to keep my eyes on. We have achieved the first two. The third is still ahead of us.

I can hardly wait.

CAPTAIN'S DOSSIER

We created history in the 2013-14 Ashes series by using the same eleven players in every Test match, with the same twelfth man, James Faulkner. To conclude my diary, I would like to say a little about each of those players:

363 runs at 40.3
2 centuries
8 catches

Chris Rogers:
463 runs at 46.3
2 centuries
3 catches

CHRIS **ROGERS**

With so many years of experience in first-class cricket yet only having played one Test match in 2008, it looked like Chris's chance had passed him by at the beginning of 2013. But the selectors recalled him for our tour of England, and what a call it was. His steadiness at the top of the order was one thing, but his steadiness in the changing room and around the team, in lots of little ways that people don't see, was equally valuable. Over the two Ashes series combined, he was Australia's top run-scorer. He made centuries in Durham, Melbourne and Sydney, and followed them with another in Port Elizabeth, South Africa. Not coincidentally, these were four of the toughest batting wickets we played on. Chris also had very good hands in the field, taking a vital outfield catch in Brisbane and a memorable leaping one in Perth.

David Warner:
523 runs at 58.11
2 centuries
3 catches

DAVID WARNER

David came of age this year. He has always had confidence in himself, but this was put to the test on the field, when he had to deal with some of the best new-ball attacks in the game. After a struggle in India and the first part of the tour of England, he blossomed in the Ashes series in Australia, topping the aggregates, and then was man of the series in South Africa, with three centuries. He always had the courage to play his way, even against the best bowling. His ability to shut the occasional off-field distraction out of his mind also spoke for his maturity and mental strength.

Shane Watson:
345 runs at 38.33
1 century
4 wickets at 30.5
2 catches

SHANE WATSON

Shane's experience was invaluable throughout the back-to-back series. He was ever-ready to help young players at training, and at first slip he was an outstanding presence and a safe pair of hands. When batting, he always put the team's needs first, even when moved around the order. His bowling was dependably accurate, invariably slowing down the scoring when we needed it, and offered vital relief to the frontline seamers. Like many of us, Shane simply grew sick of losing after the tour of India, and played in Australia with an unrelenting determination to win back the Ashes, and then keep on winning. He was injured before the First Test match in South Africa, but returned to play a key role for us in the decider, this time batting at number six.

Steve Smith:
327 runs at 40.87
2 centuries
7 catches

STEVE SMITH

At the beginning of 2013, Smithy was not in the Test team. A year later, he is one of its most important members and a key player for our future. This transformation started in India, when he made a 90 after being called up as a replacement, and he forced his way into the Ashes squad in England from the Australia A tour after not being an initial selection. He made a half-century in the first innings at Trent Bridge and went from strength to strength. His maiden Test hundred at The Oval lifted expectations again, and he played some extremely important innings in Australia, winning the man of the match award in the Perth Test match for his first-innings hundred, and scoring another first-innings century in Sydney. In South Africa, he kept that going with more runs at Centurion.

George Bailey:
183 runs at 26.14
6 catches

GEORGE BAILEY

I can't speak highly enough of George, who was the type of team man you love to have around you. People outside the group wouldn't have seen the leadership he offered behind closed doors, with his contribution to team discussions and his reading of the game. He enjoyed several highlights in the Ashes series, including his 28 runs off one James Anderson over in Perth and his maiden Test half-century in Adelaide. His catching was often outstanding. While he wasn't picked for the tour of South Africa, he continued to be a significant figure in the Australian set-up as a member of the one-day international team and captain of the Twenty20 team.

Brad Haddin:
493 runs at 61.61
1 century
22 catches

BRAD HADDIN

As vice-captain, Brad led from the front, whether with his gloves or his bat. His wicketkeeping was outstanding in the summer, with some spectacular catches and tidy work day-in, day-out. He maintained that impeccable standard in South Africa. His batting played a huge role in our 5–0 Ashes win, and he could easily have been man of the series for his century in Adelaide and his four first-innings fifties. His experience and general leadership were a mainstay of our group. Brad and I have played and trained together since we were teenagers, and I call him my partner in crime. I can't put into words how satisfying and enjoyable it has been to come through this year of cricket and win the Ashes 5-0 with Brad at my side.

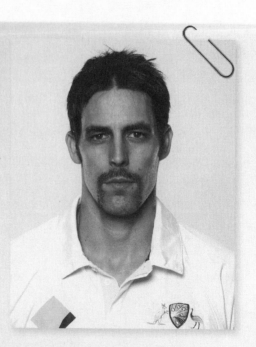

Mitchell Johnson:
37 wickets at 13.97
3 x 5W
165 runs at 27.5
4 catches
1 run outs

MITCHELL JOHNSON

What can I say that hasn't already been said? Like the whole cricket world, I was in awe of Mitch's bowling when he came back into the Test team in Australia. As his captain, I was very happy to be able to give him the ball. As a batsman, I was even happier not to have to face him. (In the nets, he was a nightmare.) When we went to South Africa, he was just as devastating against some of the best batsmen in the world. I would like to pay tribute most of all to something within Mitch – not so much the spectacular pace and talent, but the attitude and hunger he brought back with him. He had an uncompromising need for success this year. Put aside all the technical tweaks to his bowling, and this was the thing that stood out for me: his desire to succeed.

Peter Siddle:
16 wickets at 24.12
38 runs at 6.33

PETER SIDDLE

The underrated Peter Siddle played a major role in our Ashes win. Whenever we needed a breakthrough that would change the momentum of a match, or just a spell that would stop the batsmen's flow and build up pressure, Sidds was the bowler I could rely on. If you look through this diary, you will often see how the course of a match was turned in our favour by a spell from Sidds. His record against Kevin Pietersen, in particular, was a key to our being able to restrict England's scores. He slid up like a snake: England never saw him coming. What a fantastic complement to Mitch and Ryan he proved. In the team group, Sidds stepped up to a new status as a senior player, and was one of our most effective and respected leaders.

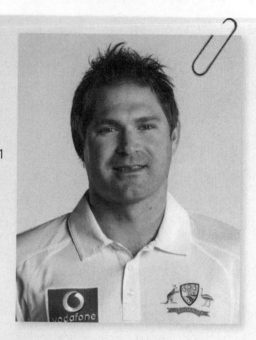

Ryan Harris:
22 wickets at 19.31
1 x 5W
117 runs at 23.4
4 catches

RYAN HARRIS

If you saw what Ryan put his body through in order to realise his dream of becoming a regular Australian Test player, you would love him as much as I do. He played through pain that would cripple many people. Always a fantastic bowler, Ryan finally achieved the recognition that was his due, with nine straight Test matches from Lord's to Sydney and then another three in South Africa. He was our best player in the first of those Ashes matches at Lord's, and our best player in the last, at Sydney. He was one of our best in every match between them. What a bowler. As a team man, he was vocal in putting Australia's interests first. His batting was important at times, and he had safe hands in many different positions in the field. In South Africa, he had a slow start but burst back into the series in Cape Town, taking the last two wickets of a super summer.

Nathan Lyon:
19 wickets at 29.36
1 x 5W
60 runs no average
5 catches

NATHAN **LYON**

This year, Nathan stepped out of Shane Warne's shadow. He is now one of the most successful Test off-spinners Australia has ever produced, so he is carving out a place in history for himself. Continually during the Ashes, Nathan stepped up to take important wickets, from Brisbane through to Sydney. He troubled England's left-handed openers, and in Melbourne he bowled a match-winning spell using the wind to his advantage on a pitch that didn't offer much spin. Also, when wickets fell at the other end, Nathan was more responsible than any other bowler, by placing pressure on the batsmen and enabling the pacemen to follow their plans. Nathan was a key to our bowling partnerships. As leader of our team song, Nathan had to wait ten Test matches before he could do it for the first time – but then it became regular work.

JAMES **FAULKNER**

James was one of many whose support for our team off the field might not have grabbed the headlines but was greatly appreciated. Twelfth man is a demanding job, and James was supportive and diligent at all times. He had his thumb cracked while batting in the nets in Perth, but he came back later in the summer with an unforgettable hitting display in our one-day win over England in Brisbane. James has a very bright future for Australia in all formats of the game.

THE SUPPORT STAFF

Darren Lehmann *Head Coach*

Craig McDermott *Bowling Coach*

Michael Di Venuto *Batting Coach*

Steve Rixon *Fielding Coach*

Mike Young *Coaching Consultant*

John Davison *Spin Bowling Coach*

Dene Hills *Performance Analyst*

Damian Mednis *Strength & Conditioning Coach*

Alex Kountouris *Physiotherapist*

Dr Peter Brukner *Team Doctor*

Gavin Dovey *Team Manager*

Grant Baldwin *Masseur & Logistics Coordinator*

Matt Cenin *Media Manager*

Kate Hutchison *Media Manager*

Frank Dimasi *Security Manager*

Michael Lloyd *Sports Psychologist*

I hesitate to single anyone out, but on a personal note I can say I would not have been able to contribute as I did to the Australian team without the dedication and skill of our physiotherapist Alex Kountouris. Often at great sacrifice, at any hour and on any day of the year, Alex would move mountains to get us into playing condition. He did this for every member of the squad, but I'm afraid I needed his help more than most. Thanks, Alex!

ACKNOWLEDGEMENTS

Captain's Diary has been a real team effort from the start. The time that my wife Kyly and great friend Warnie dedicated to writing their personal insights is very much appreciated and I believe they both add a fantastic personal insight.

As I hope to have reflected in the Diary, the results we achieved over the 2013–14 Ashes summer would not have been possible without the dedication of our support staff. Getting us onto the field in peak condition, and keeping us there through five Test matches is no mean feat and I applaud them for their efforts.

For the first time in the history of the game we used the same XI in all five Tests, so the final word of thanks goes to my teammates for their dedication, commitment and camaraderie over what was a summer I will never forget.